G000125502

"That suffering, whether in our intimate circle or on the incomprehensible scale of the Asian tsunami, is a challenge to faith in God has been comprehensively explored in writing. What makes Mark Dowd's account . . . so readable, compelling, and intimate is how he manages to capture so well both the human capacity to bear the unbearable and the nuanced, subtle part faith, against all expectations, can play in that."

—PETER STANDFORD
Author of *What We Talk about When We Talk about Faith*

"Mark Dowd invites us to accept that we are part of an evolutionary process constituted by cycles of death and renewal without denying the tragic aspect of suffering which seems to exceed any natural necessity. Dowd offers no platitudinous solution but seeks inspiration from those who embody compassion in the midst of intolerable anguish. Rather than debating the existence of God, we can draw hope from the very fact that such people exist."

—TINA BEATTIE
Author of *The Good Priest*

My Tsunami Journey

My Tsunami Journey

The Quest for God in a Broken World

Mark Dowd

Foreword by Rowan Williams

RESOURCE *Publications* · Eugene, Oregon

MY TSUNAMI JOURNEY
The Quest for God in a Broken World

Resource Publications
An Imprint of Wipf and Stock Publishers
199 W. 8th Ave., Suite 3
Eugene, OR 97401

www.wipfandstock.com

PAPERBACK ISBN: 978-1-7252-9535-3
HARDCOVER ISBN: 978-1-7252-9534-6
EBOOK ISBN: 978-1-7252-9536-0

11/16/21

"The Lepers of Mtemwa" by John Bradburne is reproduced with the permission of the John Bradburne Memorial Society

Extract from the article by William Broad, "Deadly and Yet Necessary, Earthquakes Renew the Planet", is reproduced with the permission of The New York Times

This book is dedicated to the memory of my dear father, Edward Patrick Dowd, who cannot have known that a mere five words, uttered in front of a TV set in December 2004, could have set in train an award-winning TV documentary . . . and eighteen years later . . . this book.

Contents

Foreword

EVERY GENERATION—PERHAPS EVERY DECADE—SEEMS to have its moment of cosmic doubt and trauma, some event or series of events that, just for a bit, makes it impossible to turn away from the scale of human suffering. And when this happens, the religious agonize, the irreligious point out that this confirms the meaninglessness of speaking about God, and the not-quite-sure look yearningly for something that makes sense of it all. People of my age will still remember the horror of the Aberfan disaster of 1966. For the last eighteen months or so, the Covid pandemic has been the focus for many. But the Asian tsunami of 2004 will surely be one of the things that will always stick in the mind and imagination, a loss of life within just a couple of days on a scale that leaves you numb.

Religious people are repeatedly faced with the question—angry, heartbroken, stunned—of how belief in God and trust in God (not quite the same thing) can possibly survive this level of pain and loss, let alone actually help you live with the memory of it. There are some fairly familiar ways of dealing with the challenge, and one of these is to admit that there are no cast-iron answers to the contradictions exposed, but that we might still be able to trust the experience of those whose faith *does* survive and really seems to strengthen and nourish them. But it is rare for anyone to probe this in depth. Who are these people? What do they actually say, and why? Are their responses really shaped by the religious tradition they belong to or are they the coping mechanisms that some sorts of human temperament throw up?

Mark Dowd's book has its origins in the direct challenge to faith expressed by his father in the face of the tsunami, and it undertakes just this kind of probing. It is an intensely moving record of real listening: Mark lets his own Western pieties and sensitivities be challenged by the often very alien sentiments expressed by some of those he meets, and he approaches every interviewee with respect and readiness to learn. Attempts at various kinds of theological explanation are allowed to unfold without impatient or belittling commentary—though he is willing also to be honest about where his sympathy falls. His own experience of loss and his own distinctive journey of calling and discovery are woven into a really compelling narrative. This is a book of great and transparent humanity.

It is worth a great many tomes on "the problem of suffering", and I would hope that anyone seriously trying to find ways of speaking about faith in the presence of appalling anguish will read it, more than once. If there really is not going to be an explanation that will allow us to sit back and stop worrying about it, each person will have to find a way of travelling with the painful, unresolved challenge. But as we travel, we share with one another how we are coping, how we are, just as a matter of fact, making sense, moving forward. And this attention to what people actually *do* to manage the reality of suffering is one of the things that keeps faith alive, often in very unexpected ways. Mark's story illustrates this with rare clarity and genuine depth.

Rowan Williams
July 2021

Preface and Acknowledgements

LET ME SPELL OUT the two groups which this book is probably *not* likely to appeal to. First, militant atheists who find religious language and explanation about as convincing as talk about Santa Claus and the Tooth Fairy (these analogies have always been the favorites of the scourge of the God-fearing from the self-confessed high priest of new atheism, Professor Richard Dawkins). The second group consists of believers so convinced of God's goodness that the troubling waves of doubt which afflict so many of the rest of us make next to no impact on the manner in which they conduct their lives. Often accompanying this outlook on the world is a quasi-literal interpretation of the Holy Scriptures. In these two communities we have very different people. But neither is especially bothered by the question "how has God created a world in which little babies can die of leukemia?"

No, this book is specifically aimed at two other groups of people: troubled believers (count me in, most certainly, here) and agnostics who in their heart of hearts wish to make a crucial next step of assent to faith but for whom the whole question of the apparent incompatibility of the existence of a good God and the presence of death and suffering in the world prevents them from making that decisive life-changing commitment.

This book was born out of a few words spoken to me by my father on December 26, 2004. It was, in effect, almost the last utterance he spoke to me in person before he died just a few weeks later. So it is deeply fitting that I dedicate this book to his memory. But there are dozens more who must be mentioned. The production team at 3BMTV who were so key to making the documentary on which this work is based: Charlie Hawes, Bruno Sorrentino, Jessica Ross, Marion Milne, and Simon Ardizzone, all based in the UK. And then out in the field on location in Indonesia, Thailand, India, and Portugal: Tino Saroengallo, Fauzan Uazah, Suppatra Vimonsuknopparat, Neelima Goel, Sandra Leitao, Nandha Kumar, and Subbu Subramanian.

Publishers Wipf and Stock are owed huge thanks for accepting my proposal and making a firm commitment to taking this into print. I also have to thank the following who either made comments on the text or came up with ideas and insights of their own which influenced the composition of the later sections of this work: Philip Clayton, David Crystal, Julian Filochowski, Patrick Geary, Joanne Hinchliffe, Father Timothy Radcliffe OP, and Didier Rance. In particular I owe a special debt of gratitude to the former Archbishop of Canterbury, Dr Rowan Williams, who kindly accepted an invitation to write a foreword to this book without hesitation. As an admirer of his writings and preaching for many years, it is a deep honor which I shall always treasure.

My agent, Bill Goodall, performed sterling work with formatting the first draft of my manuscript, as did Isabella Michon at IM Media Inc who took on the task of promoting this work far and wide in the press and media with exactly the right combination of energy, integrity and appreciation for my book's subject matter.

To my husband, Stephen Gingell, who patiently sat through hours of my musing and commenting on the development of this book as it took shape. Thank you for indulging me and listening to my hours of meanderings.

Finally, approximately 230,000 people lost their lives in the Indian Ocean tsunami of December 2004. May their memories live on vibrantly with those families and friends they left behind.

May their souls be granted rest.

The Genesis of My Tsunami Journey

THE PICTURESQUE PEAK DISTRICT in the north of England is a most un-usual location from where to launch a "Tsunami Journey". This area of outstanding natural beauty covers more than five hundred square miles, and its hills and dales provide limitless opportunities for recreation for thousands of families in the nearby post-industrial cities of Manchester, Sheffield, and Nottingham. In the December of 2004, I had rented a very cute cottage in the charming village of Grindleford in the Derwent Valley. In the days prior to Christmas, I had got all the food in and duly invited my parents to drive down from Manchester and join me after my long drive up from London. Years of work as a television documentary maker had meant that family reunions like this were few and far between. For once, work would not intervene. This was to be quality time.

As traditional Catholics we had taken in midnight mass at a nearby church, consumed our Christmas Day turkey with all the customary trimmings and washed it all down with a bottle or two of decent Spanish Rioja. There was ample time for catch-up with detailed updates on my many relatives and all the tittle-tattle of life in their Manchester parish. On Boxing Day, in order to cast off the cobwebs, I took to the hills and ended up doing an exhilarating ten-mile hike along Curbar Edge, taking in the picturesque villages of Baslow and Frogatt. Early evening and the turkey re-appeared, this time in the form of a very tasty curry which my mother had been marinating all day. More wine. More chat. Then at 9 pm, Dad switched on the

TV (if I had had my way I'd have hidden the contraption as I used to hate the way excessively loud television often spoiled family Christmases, but there was no harm in watching for a few minutes).

"Let's see what's going on in the world?" said Dad. "That's the thing with Christmas, you tend to get cut off from things a bit."

We'd actually joined the BBC News 24 bulletin a minute or two late and had missed the studio introduction, so as the images of the main report came into focus we heard the following:

"This was Sri Lanka as the seawater flooded inland," intoned the reporter to the pictures of cars and boats being hurled down streets by raging torrents of water. "Thousands have lost their lives here. Government officials say that one million people, around 5 percent of the island's population, have been affected."[1]

Worse was to follow. As the cobbled-together footage from the different affected countries landed on our screen, a solitary image of a young father wading through the water with his lifeless infant now punctured the peace of our Yuletide family gathering. When the focus finally switched to Sumatra, the Indonesian island closest to the epicenter of this tumultuous seismic event, the commentary talked about "four thousand estimated fatalities". The eventual recorded death toll of the "Indian Ocean Boxing Day Tsunami" as it came to be called, turned out to be 227,898.[2] Within days, this largely unknown three-syllabled Japanese word, translated as "harbor wave", became an everyday word on people's lips the world over.

The news report left us in shock. My father got up to switch the TV off. After a long silence, I gazed over towards my parents who were sitting on the cherry-colored sofa directly opposite the television. I'm not sure what I was expecting them to say, but amongst all the candidates for phrases likely to follow such a disturbing broadcast, I had not counted on the following from my father.

"God could have stopped that."

"What?" I thought to myself.

I took it up with him.

"Dad, I know what you mean, but you can't have a world in which God is being called upon to act like a magician every time nature gets a bit out of hand. I mean, the natural world behaves according to the principles of

1. BBC News 24 Bulletin, evening of December 26, 2004.

2. http://itic.ioc-unesco.org/index.php?option=com_content&view=category&id=1136&Itemid=1373.

science. If God intervenes some of the time but not others, you don't have a world that behaves predictably and what would be the point of studying all the laws of science?"

Another long silence. My mother looked more than a little nervous as she sensed the rising tension in the small living room.

"Why do we pray for God to cure people then?" my father countered. "Jesus helped the lame to walk again and the blind to see. Isn't that intervening in things?"

This was threatening to get heavy. We hadn't talked like this in years.

"Aren't these miracle stories in the Gospels about the faith and response of people to the presence of Jesus?" I said. I knew I was floundering. Was I really implying that if all the people threatened by those colossal waves had had similar faith in the Son of God, they would have been spared?

I had rarely exchanged bitter words with my father. But then he fixed a stare.

"You've always got an answer, haven't you?" he said.

The Catholic faith was in the DNA of our family and had been a hitherto unquestioned bond between me and my parents. At the age of eight I had been an altar boy at our local church and my father would often get me up early for mass before he went off on his shift work on the buses. My mother had been a stalwart in the UCM, The Union of Catholic Mothers. She sang in the parish choir while my father took occupation of his little table at the rear of the church, handing out hymn books and organizing the collection. Weekly dance nights in the parish hall were a staple diet of their social life. In short, this wasn't just about assenting to a series of abstract theological propositions. This was an entire way of life, their identity.

That night I barely slept. Partly because I kept seeing all those distressing images from the TV reports in my mind and partly because I kept replaying, again and again, that very strained and awkward conversation with my father. *"You've always got an answer haven't you?"* Nothing could be further from the truth. The painfully slow hours of the night prompted uncomfortable flashbacks. First to university. In 1978, aged eighteen, I had left the security of my Catholic school and home and gone to Exeter in the south-west of England to read politics. I attended mass regularly, even becoming the liturgy representative on the Catholic Society Committee. But numerous challenging conversations among fellow students in the late-night hours after far too many beers had never really gone away after twenty-five years or more:

3

"You say you're a Christian. Why then has God made a world in which innocent little babies die of leukemia?"

"Why didn't God intervene and stop the Holocaust if the Jews were his chosen people?"

"You say God is all-loving and omnipotent? Why then has he made such a botched job of creation with so much disease, suffering and death?"

I'd occasionally posed these questions at secondary (high) school to my religious studies teachers and, more often than not, I'd been fobbed off with answers of the "it's an inscrutable mystery" variety. Well if so, it was a mystery that was causing my seventy-six-year-old father to fundamentally question his faith. It had been these troubling unresolved questions which had propelled me, at the age of twenty-one, into the Dominican Order in Oxford. The Order of Preachers, as they were known, are renowned scholars and intellectuals. It is not surprising that any group of thinkers and writers that boasted St Thomas Aquinas in their ranks could lay claim to some of the finest theologians in the Christian world and they were happy to accept the request of a restless and curious graduate. Alongside the attention to scriptures and philosophy, I took time off to read some of the heavyweights in this area of God and Evil: John Hick, Richard Swinburne, and Alvin Plantinga. There was even one of the friars, Father Brian Davies OP, who devoted much of his lecturing to the knotty problems of God and a less than perfect world. Why I did not pursue my vocation to the priesthood after a stay of eighteen months is a long and protracted tale. But by the time I left Blackfriars Priory in 1983, I had made some form of progress, at least so I thought. The so-called "Free Will Defense", espoused classically by John Hick, had partially at least given a reasonable riposte. God values absolute human autonomy for the human family. So much so, that wars, torture, rape, and human cruelty were essentially misuses of freedom and the heavy price we paid for genuine freedom. If God stepped in every time we chose badly, we would be reduced to automatons, and an all-loving Creator wishes his creatures to choose goodness for its own sake, not because they have been pre-programmed to do so. No, what was unresolved for me was so-called "natural evil" (a problematic term I concede, since earthquakes and diseases like Covid-19 are not moral agents making ethical choices based on complex criteria). Perhaps a better, albeit long-winded, term would be "the barbed wire and booby traps of nature that have deleterious consequences for human beings". I am not sure this will ever catch on, but I hope, dear reader, you get my drift?

I pondered, once more, the previous night's TV map that had relayed to us which areas had been affected. Sri Lanka and Thailand with their huge Buddhist populations. Hindus, Muslims, and Christians in India and in Indonesia, in population terms the largest state in the world to practice the Islamic faith. What were all these people making of the suffering of innocent people, of creation, of God's role in it all? I realized I knew next to nothing about what these great belief systems had to say on the subject. Then, a truly undeniable "Eureka" moment. Why not make a huge television film and explore just that, a two-hour epic, with visits to the affected territories and interviews with people on the ground?

After breakfast I called Aaqil Ahmed, head of religious programming at Channel Four TV at his offices in Horseferry Road in Westminster, central London. I had made a three-part series for him in the spring of 2004 which looked at faith in the post 9/11 world. It was called *Children of Abraham* and it had been very well received by the Channel Four hierarchy and had even picked up an award or two.[3] I explained to him what had happened with my father, my near sleepless night and why it would make an absolutely gripping "watch" on the box. He listened to my excited program pitch patiently.

"Look," he said, "I can totally see why this would make a gripping one-off documentary, but it's December 27. There's no one around much to get an answer from. I can't commission something of this size and scope without getting an OK from Kevin." Kevin Lygo was Director of Television and Content at Channel Four and one of the most influential people in the UK television industry. Aaqil ended the call, promising his best. Now, I've had sufficient years of experience in the TV world to appreciate the saint-like patience required to move successfully from the early germination of a program idea to its eventual commission with an attendant budget, schedule, and broadcast date. It often required endless meetings, re-workings of ideas and, increasingly in the current age, the inclusion of a celebrity name or two to jazz up the appeal and guarantee an audience. Religious broadcasting was often allowed exceptional status from these commercial pressures as legal statutes placed obligations on television moguls to deliver a required minimum number of hours broadcasting a year. No one expected you to get an audience of five million for a transmission on faith and fundamentalism. The result was that, more often than not, your programs were

---

3. *Children of Abraham*: 3BMTV Productions for Channel Four TV: a three-part series which aired in the UK in April and May 2004.

sacrificed in slots against hugely popular offerings on other channels. It was frequently a bloodbath, and if you got a 5 percent share of the audience across the five main terrestrial channels, you were lucky.

That then, was the context in which, only two hours later, Aaqil called me back on my mobile:

"Listen, I got hold of Kevin. We're on! A two-hour anniversary documentary for Christmas 2005. Budget of around £250,000 [$350,000]." I was flabbergasted. Never had the TV world acted at such speed.

As soon as I had finished with Aaqil, I was eager to break the news of the documentary to my parents. I, perhaps naively, had assumed that it might smooth things over after the charged exchanges of the night before. "Well Dad, at least our discussion has had a major spin-off," I said with a beam on my face, "you've just got me the best part of a year's work." I explained to him how I had recapped fragments of our conversation with the Channel Four program chief. However, my father, never one for basking in the limelight, in contrast to his middle son, just looked at me and carried on pouring the tea. It was my mother who reacted more animatedly.

"Does that mean you'll be going to all these places that have been damaged?" she asked with a furrow on her brow. I knew the subtext of this question. It wasn't excitement over journalistic enquiry. It was understandable maternal anxiety. My poor mother. I had frequently scared the life out of her in some of my assignments. The Oklahoma bombing of 1995, frequent trips to Northern Ireland during the terror-strewn "troubles", and the one she eventually really freaked out over; a confrontation with a balaclava-clad member of Islamic Jihad on the back streets of Gaza for a program called The Fundamentalists.[4] She did have a point. He was brandishing his AK-47 rather menacingly throughout the course of the interview, and the news that the BBC Middle East correspondent, Alan Johnson, had recently been abducted just a mile or two away did make this one of the hairier missions I had undertaken.[5] None of this I related to her at the time. She only saw the eventual evidence on screen. The result of my sincerely intentioned desire to protect her was to make her ever more anxious when a project got under way because she (rightly) concluded I was being less than forthright with the nature of the potential hazards ahead.

---

4. The Fundamentalists: October Films for Channel Four TV, September 9, 2006.

5. Alan Johnson, BBC reporter, was abducted by a group calling itself The Army of Islam and was released on July 4, 2007, after 114 days in captivity.

"Mum, don't worry. By the time we get out there I'm sure all the threat of earthquake aftershocks will have died down," I said, trying to console her. The tsunami had been precipitated by one of the most powerful earthquakes known since records began, measuring 9.1 on the Richter scale, with some of the waves reportedly reaching nine meters in height by the time they hit the shoreline. It had unleashed twice the amount of energy in all the bombs utilized in World War Two.[6] Its pinpoint epicenter was located at latitude 3.30 degrees north of the equator and longitude 95.98 degrees east[7] and ranked third in the all-time recorded list of powerful earthquakes. At a Richter rating of 9.5, it's unlikely that the 1960 Valdivia tremor in southern Chile will ever be surpassed. However, despite its superior force, the South American death toll was placed at "only" 1,655 people compared to the near 230,000 individuals who lost their lives in December 2004.[8] The fact is that the underpinning infrastructure of houses and buildings in Sumatra, coastal India, Thailand, and Sri Lanka was decisively feeble in comparison. We might rail at God for the faulty design of his creation, but humans too bear some responsibility when it comes to important choices about investment and making sure the most vulnerable are afforded as much protection as the wealthy and powerful.

The day after the news of our television commission, it was time to part company with my parents. There were the customary hugs and kisses from mother and a rather less showy farewell from my father who wound down the window of their postbox-red Mini Metro hatchback. "Thanks for a nice time and a nice Christmas, love," he said. "We'll call you when we get home just to let you know we've made it back safely. It shouldn't be more than two hours from here," he said as my mother put the car into gear. I waved them off. Their miniscule vehicle meandered along the tiny high street of Grindleford and disappeared over the hill at the end of the village.

The next time I was to see my father, he was jaundiced and motionless, laid out in the chapel of rest at Barlow's undertakers just a five-minute walk from the family home. The Tsunami documentary had, effectively, been his parting gift to me.

---

6. https://www.britannica.com/event/Indian-Ocean-tsunami-of-2004.

7. https://www.usgs.gov/natural-hazards/earthquake-hazards/science/20-largest-earthquakes-world?qt-science_center_objects=0#qt-science_center_objects.

8. https://earthquake.usgs.gov/earthquakes/eventpage/official19600522191120_30/impact.

The ensuing days after the numbing images of the Indian Ocean tsunami only served to justify Channel Four's decision to go ahead with the film. I was a little uneasy that a lot of the media attention had focused on the plight of western tourists trapped in hotels at the expense of local people who didn't have the option to get out their credit cards and fly out of the disaster zone. Secondary effects were now becoming apparent. Eruptions of typhoid and cholera due to severely compromised sanitation systems. Shortages of food and clothing for people who were living in piles of rubble. Day after day, the newspapers were flooded with huge disaster appeal advertisements from Oxfam, the Red Cross and an organization called the DEC, the Disasters Emergencies Committee.[9]

In the midst of all this fallout, the press now began to look for new angles and found one in a piece commissioned for the Sunday Telegraph. The author was none other than Dr Rowan Williams, the Archbishop of Canterbury. "This has made me question God's existence" screamed the headlines on the first Sunday of the new year.[10] Not for the first or last time, the sub-editors had been a bit indulgent with their choice of words for the front page splash. What Dr Williams had actually said was that it was right and appropriate to ask where God was in all this and conceded that he could understand how *other people* might have their faith disturbed by such events. He wasn't announcing his intention to join Richard Dawkins, Christopher Hitchens, Sam Harris, and Daniel Dennet, the so-called "Four Horsemen of New Atheism", by his newspaper article, despite the best efforts of Fleet Street's print editors to generate as much controversy as they could. In a subsequent Tsunami Service of Remembrance held at St Paul's Cathedral in London, the Archbishop went on to cite a well-known English post-war poet:

"Philip Larkin said, 'What will survive of us is love'; but this is true not only in the rather wistful sense that the memory of love survives when other things about us have been forgotten. It is true in the sense that love can continue to grow even on the soil of the worst pain and the deepest doubt. When we stretch and torment our minds over the problem of evil in the world, we should not forget that the survival of love is just as much of a mystery."[11]

9. https://en.wikipedia.org/wiki/Disasters_Emergency_Committee.

10. https://www.telegraph.co.uk/news/uknews/1480232/Archbishop-of-Canterbury-This-has-made-me-question-Gods-existence.html.

11. Tsunami 2004: A Service of Remembrance. St Paul's Cathedral May 11, 2005.

I comprehended easily enough the first part of the Archbishop's statement, but the second bit left me somewhat confused. Why is the survival of love a *mystery*? It would take me only a few months, with direct experience of witnessing the turmoil and aftermath of the tsunami waves, to begin to get an inkling of what Dr Williams had in mind.

The siren voices of competing positions on the "God and Natural Disasters" debate were not slow to take their gloves off. Arch-atheist and author of *The God Delusion*, Oxford biologist Richard Dawkins, wasn't slow to use the discomfort of believers to add grist to his mill. In a letter, in a prominent national broadsheet, he wrote:

"It is psychologically possible to derive some comfort from sincere belief in a non-existent illusion. But—silly me—I thought believers might be disillusioned with an omnipotent being who had just drowned 125,000 people."[12]

In the ensuing weeks, as we gathered together the team which would research, shoot, and edit the eventual mammoth documentary, I placed Richard Dawkins high on my list of early would-be interviewees. I confess to being really irked by interventions such as his. It was bad enough feeling the cognitive dissonance of trying to hold on to faith in the midst of the appalling suffering out in the Indian Ocean, but to have letters such as his, mischievously taunting people like me and, to my mind at least, "using" tragedy as an opportunistic tool to advance his case was a bit beyond the pale. Mine was probably an overreaction, a sure enough sign that his needling had indeed struck a very painful chord.

Dawkins was in the final throes of finishing off his book when I went to see him at his home in north Oxford. Never one to shun exposure and the press, he was especially keen to talk as he had his potential bestseller to promote. As my cameraman and friend, Bruno Sorrentino and I, sauntered up the leafy wide streets of Parktown, a very plush area less than a mile north of many of the university's major science buildings, I scanned all the huge detached late Victorian houses and felt the familiar attack of "imposter syndrome". I was born into a very working-class family. My devoted and loving dad had worked first on night shifts on a production line making aircraft parts and then, latterly, as a bus conductor with LUT: Lancashire United Transport. My mother, since the age of fifteen, had worked in a dress shop, initially as an assistant, then managing it and eventually going on to run her own business. We had a council house in post-industrial Salford where

12. *The Guardian*, January 1, 2005.

9

the artist L.S. Lowry had made his reputation with his haunting paintings of cloth-capped men trudging their way to work amidst the smokestacks and overbearing factory buildings. Our modest house was owned by the local municipality to whom we paid a monthly rent. In a different generation, with a different roll of the dice, my parents would both have made it to university, but this was not to be in the post-war late 1940s. And here I was, looking at these grand houses in Oxford worth about a million-and-a-half-pounds each and getting ever so slightly nervous. What on earth was *I* doing here? Dawkins was no fool, I knew that. Was he just going to make mincemeat of me, run rings around my points of view and leave me feeling deflated before the project had even got under way?

When I had seen him on TV, the prize-winning biologist had often come across as rather cold and aloof, but as he welcomed us into his home, he was the epitome of kindness. Coffee was brought into an enormous lounge with very extensive windows looking out onto a large and very well-maintained rear garden. We were left here for about half an hour to set up the camera and lights. When we were ready, we signaled to his assistant that we were ready to start. It's a hallmark of Dawkins' supreme self confidence that he had requested very little information or background about the documentary we were making. I had simply found his email details on an Oxford University website, taken a phone call from his assistant and agreed a time and date. Once the camera started up, he was quick out of his tracks.

"It's a kind of human vanity, as some religious people do," he said coolly, "that this is a kind of revenge from God, or a warning from God or to bother our heads asking 'where was God or why was God being so evil?' The fact is that he's not there."

"Is there somewhere, "I asked him, "in a small part of your mind, a part of you that enjoys the intellectual discomfort that believers have when an event like this happens?"

He took a few seconds to think and then came back at me.

"No. I wouldn't say that. Certainly not. I want people to stop being believers. I want people to see the nonsense they believe."

No pulling punches here then. But if *I* was racked with doubts at this point, I was reluctant to walk away from his Oxford home without pressing *him* a bit further on his own position. This aura of certainty that he projected was something I wanted to explore further. I asked him to fast forward to his death bed. Ten seconds before he died, knowing that the physical world he had lived in had no self-generating explanation for its own existence, would he not have a few lingering doubts; just a little *wobble* about the God question?

"I don't think the fact that I was just about to die would have anything to do with it," he said. "I would certainly have wobbles about my capacity to understand the Universe. Good heavens, that's an enormous deep, deep question. And who I am to say that I understand it? Of course I don't understand it."

But then, out of the blue, came an elaboration to his answer which almost made me fall off the sofa.

"But the kind of God I would respect people for believing in would be the kind of God of the Deists[13] who set up the Universe in the first place, who set up laws of physics that could bring the conditions for evolution to come into existence. But that is not the kind of God of the physicists who would be the slightest bit interested in listening to the odd prayer."

For a man who was in the last stages of launching his vituperative *The God Delusion* on the outside world, this was quite a concession. "*The kind of God I would respect people for believing in . . .*" was not a gambit I had at all expected. And this is the classic Deist position. A God who is the "first cause", who brings about the physical world but who is then remote and unengaged with it. It's a far cry from the Christian orthodoxy of incarnation which suggests that not only does God underpin and hold creation in his very being at all times, but that God actually became part of the physical world by taking on human flesh in his son Jesus, to redeem humanity and the world in an act of loving surrender.

At the end of our conversation, the Oxford professor left us to wrap up our lights and recording equipment and prepare to leave. We shook hands. "Thank you," he said. "Let me know when you are ready to leave. I'd like a final word before you go." My cameraman Bruno and I exchanged looks. What did he want to say?

Fifteen minutes later, we headed down the long corridor towards the front door. "So can I ask you bluntly," came a voice behind me. "As you seem quite an intelligent person, I take it you still believe in God? Tell me, I'm curious. What are the reasons for your faith?" I had seen Dawkins many times on TV, offering analogies between belief in God and belief in the Tooth

13. The Deists were a group of freethinking Europeans of the eighteenth century. Their general view was to accept a God who set up the laws on which the scientific world operated but then remained indifferent to creation. Deists do not accept the supernaturally inspired divine revelation through the Bible and other texts, but insist on the primacy of human reason.

Fairy or Santa Claus. Was this the kind of hurried discussion I should be having in a cramped corridor in a house in north Oxford? I put down the filming equipment I was holding.

"Well," I said, "I note how you pit intelligence against faith and remind you that many great scientists have found space for God in their deliberations."

"Yes, I know that," he retorted. "But I want to know what *your* reasons are." I felt Bruno's eyes on me and took a deep breath.

"Two main reasons," I said. "First, as the universe does not contain within itself the reason for its own existence, there is a contingency question. How did all this come about? I can't accept The Big Bang just started out of nothing . . . and before you counter with 'what created God?', it's always been a position of Christian orthodoxy that God is not another 'thing in the universe', therefore asking what caused God is a wrong-category question like asking if bananas are sadder than pineapples." I couldn't believe I was talking like this to him, but he had started it! "So, I just think it begs a question," I continued, "It's not a proof for God, just it opens up a space for enquiry." Dawkins had a knowing smile on his face and then asked me what my second reason was. "I'd say I have met, in my lifetime, a very small number of people who exude what I would call 'a peace that surpasseth all understanding.'"[14] He looked at me attentively. "They have a sense of great calm and holiness about them and that always seems to be rooted in a profound sense of the sacred."

I was expecting a riposte and the beginning of a lengthy discussion. But he just looked at me and held his gaze. "Hmm. Interesting. Well, off you go now. Safe trip." And that, was that. The first Tsunami interview in the can and we had not even left the Home Counties.

It was now early February and research was continuing at great pace. Our plan was to travel out to the Indian Ocean in late April and the fledgling production team was on the job trying to secure the assistance of location producers in Thailand, India, and Indonesia and find a spectrum of human stories. I spent hours and hours in the British Library off Euston Road in central London, trying to get a handle on what the great faiths of Buddhism, Hinduism, and Islam all had to say about human suffering and the God question. I had expected to find dozens of learned tomes with a penetrating comparative religion angle on this most pressing of questions, but instead, I found just one solitary book with an overarching treatment

14. The phrase comes from Phil 4:7.

of the issue. *The Problems of Suffering in the Religions of the World* by Anglican priest and theologian, John Bowker. I was genuinely shocked that so little attention had been paid to this area of enquiry beyond the traditional Christian "theodicy" viewpoint. That very word, "theodicy", first coined by the German philosopher Gottfried Wilhelm Leibniz in a series of French essays in 1710, had come to be widely used for the exercise of justifying God in the light of his less than perfect creation.[15] Seeing this name provoked multiple flashbacks to high school in the late 1970s and our study of Voltaire's superb 1759 classic satire, *Candide*. Trudging around the ruins and corpses of Lisbon after the horrendous 1755 All Saint's Day earthquake, our innocent and gullible hero is treated to the constant empty refrain of his mentor, Professor Pangloss: "*Tout est pour le mieux dans le meilleur des mondes possibles*,"—"Everything is for the best in the best of possible worlds."[16]

Through his pillorying of Pangloss's mindless optimism, Voltaire is implicitly merciless in his treatment of Leibniz's theodicy, that if God is indeed good, then this created world must be the very best model on offer. Acquainting myself with all this again now gave me an idea. Before our travels to the wreckages of the tsunami zone, I wanted to do one more interview.

And I wanted to know the answer to one simple question. If you're a Christian, couldn't all these imperfections in nature which led to human suffering be blamed on the Fall? Our Bible tells us in the early chapters of Genesis that due to disobedience, our ancestors Adam and Eve were condemned to lose the idyllic Garden of Eden:

"Because you listened to your wife and ate fruit from the tree about which I commanded you 'You must not eat from it,'" says Yahweh. "Cursed is the ground because of you; through painful toil you will eat food from it all the days of your life. It will produce thorns and thistles for you, and you will eat the plants of the field. By the sweat of your brow you will eat your food until you return to the ground, since from it you were taken; for dust you are and to dust you will return."[17]

These last words are well known to Roman Catholics. We hear them on the first day of Lent every year at the Ash Wednesday service. By this reading from Genesis, pain and death come into the world for the human

15. Leibniz, *Essays of Theodicy*.

16. Voltaire, *Candide*, 4.

17. Gen 3:17–19 NIV.

family as a result of rebellion. It's all because our forebears didn't keep their part of the contract, right? Well, to read some Christians, you'd think that really is a sufficient explanation. In a feat of great publication haste, Oxford University mathematician Dr John Lennox got *Where is God in a Coronavirus World?* into print by the second week of April 2020. Dr Lennox has taken on the likes of Richard Dawkins and Christopher Hitchens in public on many an occasion and is an individual who traditionally rides the twin horses of scientific enquiry and religious faith impressively. Lennox cites Genesis chapter three and human rebellion as a key factor. He asserts that original sin is an adequate explanation for the existence of disease and death, as the moral corruption of our forebears "meant that God's very good creation became flawed and fractured".[18] But is this explanation adequate?

I wanted to test this with another man who has straddled the worlds of science and faith throughout the course of his lifetime. Sir John Polkinghorne isn't just a Cambridge University physicist and a knight of the realm, he is also an ordained Anglican priest and has written more than twenty-six books on the relationship between science and religion. I persuaded him to travel to Lisbon, scene of that horrendous 1755 earthquake which claimed the lives of thousands of the faithful while they were at prayer in the city's cathedral on All Saint's Day, November 1. We wandered through church ruins and up and down Lisbon's famously demanding steep streets. Then, in the Portuguese capital's Museum of Ancient Art we examined, together, an oil-on-canvas depiction of the events by João Glama Ströberle. *The Lisbon Earthquake* was composed in 1760 and captures the chaos of an event that claimed anywhere between ten thousand and a hundred thousand lives. In the center of the painting, lying in the rubble of the demolished cathedral, is a man in clerical vestments who is looking up to the heavens. "Why O Lord, why?" are the words that emanate from his plaintive expression. High above are angels wielding swords, ready to strike against the unrepentant. It is an unforgiving and harsh view of the supernatural. So, did Sir John, as a paid-up Christian, buy the idea that scenes such as this were all down to human revolt against God?

"No, I don't buy that. I certainly don't buy it as a scientist either. I mean, that a literal reading of Genesis chapter three would make you think, yes, Adam and Eve made a bad mistake and that spoiled creation. Thistles began to grow which hadn't grown there before.

18. Lennox, *Where Is God*, 40.

"But we know enough about the history of the world to know that death and disaster have been around a long, long time before there were any human beings."

Unless you are one of those creationists who believes in the literal version of creation events and that God really fashioned the planet in a period of seven days, it struck me that Sir John was spot on. I know too much about fossil records, Darwin, and yes, I've even had to read Richard Dawkins' *The Selfish Gene*. Evolution is the process by which complex biological entities like Homo sapiens came about over millions of years and death and disease is an essential and integral part of a process whereby weak genes are eliminated through natural selection. Long before humans suffered, thousands of animals and creatures were part of this whole steady process of creation and destruction and renewal. Perhaps this is what St Paul had in mind in his Letter to the Romans when he cites the "groaning as in the pains of childbirth, right up to the present time".[19]

So, I put it to Sir John, if the original sin of our biblical parents was an inadequate explanation, what was his "defense" for God, as an ordained Anglican minister? He took a few seconds and then cited the work of another Christian scientist.

"An Oxford theologian, Austin Farrer, once said 'what was God's will in the Lisbon earthquake?' and Farrer's answer is a hard one but I think a true one. Farrer's answer was that the elements of the earth's crust should behave in accordance with their nature. They are allowed to be, in their way, just as you and I are allowed to be, in our way. I call that the 'free-process defense', that God allows creatures, all forms of creatures, to be themselves."

Farrer had been warden of Keble College, Oxford in the 1960s and a firm friend of C.S. Lewis to whom he took the last sacraments on his death bed. Renowned as a fine preacher, Farrer had been raised in the Baptist faith by his father who was an enthusiastic minister, but at Oxford his son went on to embrace Anglicanism. Polkinghorne's quotation of his words rather passed me by in our conversation. This "free process defense" in which the earth's crust "behaved in accordance with its own nature" sounded like a very elaborate way of saying, "it is what it is". I could see that human creatures had to be given genuine autonomy and that moral evil was the inevitable price to be paid for the abuse of a freely given gift. But it seemed a little far-fetched to extend this analogy to inanimate aspects of the natural world. Humans had to make ethical choices and work out the correct courses of

19. Rom 8:22 NIV.

actions, hence the importance of God bestowing freedom on his subjects as a genuine act of love. But an earthquake, a virus, or other features of the natural world did not have moral agency. It did not make sense to talk of a tectonic plate behaving virtuously or a set of genes being steeped in positive ethical qualities. Maybe I had missed the point, not pressed hard enough for a clearer explanation, but as I bade farewell to the impressive Sir John, I felt a certain ambiguity. He had put me right off the whole simplistic punitive explanation for the occurrence of natural disasters derived from the Book of Genesis. But I was still left with the question that my father's spontaneous Boxing Day utterances had set in motion.

Seven weeks after he had effectively sparked off a two-hour investigation into the goodness of God with his surprising outburst, my father was now in a much more carefree mode. He was on Lanzarote in the Canary Islands with my mother. The pair of them had never so much been on a plane together until they were in their late fifties, but now having discovered the joys of winter sun, their month in a Lanzarote timeshare apartment had become a staple diet of their post-retirement lives. The chilly gloom of Manchester in early February is not everyone's first choice for raising the human spirit. One could hardly blame them. They had joined the army of working-class people in the 1970s and 1980s who had discovered airports and economy plane tickets. They had worked hard all their lives and brought up three boys. Good luck to them.

When they went away we rarely, if ever, talked on the phone. I left them to enjoy themselves. All the more unnerving then to get a voicemail message on my mobile phone one evening from my mother. "Hello love, it's only me. Er . . . nothing to get worried about but your dad's had a bit of a flutter. His heart. They're doing some checks and tests but he's sitting up in bed and eating OK. As I said, no need to worry."

I called her back and then after we had chatted, spoke to my younger brother Antony, an experienced doctor. He explained that they were going to carry out some procedures to lessen the pressure on his heart. "I'm a bit concerned for Mum out there on her own. It may not be totally necessary, but I think I should go out there just in case," he said to me. He came down to stay with me in London and took an early flight out next morning from Gatwick airport.

His intuition had been spot on. Three days later, my father died of a cardiac arrest in Arrecife General Hospital. He was seventy-six years old and had departed the earth in style since not only was it St Valentine's Day, it was also my parents' fifty-second wedding anniversary. "I think that's your dad saying he doesn't want to be forgotten," quipped my mother on the phone. I was eternally grateful that my brother had acted on his feelings as it would have been traumatic for my mother to have undergone all that on her own away from home. It took the Spanish authorities nearly three weeks to repatriate the body. The delay in planning the funeral was driving my mother mad. Even worse, the coroner in Manchester, not satisfied with the explanation and medical report he had received, wanted to carry out a post-mortem, and someone from the immediate family was now required to visit the chapel of rest where he was laid out and identify him before signing a document of consent for more medical examinations. I never told my mother as I stole off to the funeral directors. Identifying a dead body some twenty days after death is among one of the less pleasant experiences I have had to undergo in this life.

My father's unexpected death affected me more than I let on. Too many unresolved questions in our relationship. Apart from a cursory rushed phone call to the hospital bedside in Arrecife, there had been no chance to say goodbye. For days after his funeral I felt the pulsing waves of grief building up in my body. They would release themselves in the most inopportune places: at bus stops, inside bookshops, or in the middle of a chat in the pub. But as I somehow got through all this, it made me more determined than ever to plough on with the film. I used the peculiar energy unleashed by bereavement in the weeks ahead, as our small production team began to try and apply some shape and coherence for what was going to be a mammoth film shoot. We were going to be away for the best part of six weeks in Indonesia, India, and Thailand. Contrary to what most members of the viewing public may assume, the interviewees and scenes that appear in television documentary films do not just fall magically into place by a feat of serendipity. We had three location producers on the ground in the countries where we would be filming, but they needed guidance from us. Where did we want to travel to? Who did we want to interview? Endless logistical preparations: visas, health and safety forms, injections and vaccinations, who would translate for us? How would we get around? In a large communal vehicle? If so, who would be driving? In Aceh in Sumatra, how much of the area we wanted to visit would even be passable, given the manner in which the destructive wave had wrecked the landscape? Moreover, there were huge editorial issues to take into consideration. We would need a rich mixture of theological experts as well as individual human stories. I asked our people on the ground to try and find stories of people who had both had their faith strengthened as a result of their trials and also people whose belief in God had collapsed as a consequence of their ordeal. Then we would also need "the great and the good", the learned women and men who could enlighten me more about suffering and its role in the world view of their religious faith.

In preparation for these encounters, I'd need to get myself up to speed on what Islam, Hinduism, and Buddhism had to say about human suffering in the world. There is nothing worse when you are interviewing some great guru when he or she starts making reference to terms and themes which you have never heard of, or your ignorance is betrayed by the very nature of your question. So, for weeks on end before we departed for the Indian Ocean, I incarcerated myself inside that huge library just north of the Marylebone Road in London and surrounded myself with large tomes. Commentaries on the Hindu Vedas and the Upanishads, on the Qur'an and very large numbers of books on the concept of *dukkha*, or suffering, in Buddhism. As far as I was aware, no radio or television documentary had ever taken this question head on across so many different faith traditions. True enough, since 1945 Jews and others had understandably raised questions about the goodness of God in the light of the *Shoah* or Holocaust, but I wasn't aware of one single event that had cut across so many religious faiths at the same time.

Of course, it wasn't just preparation on editorial matters that required our attention. When these TV films hit the air, the average viewer knows little, if anything, about what is required before even the first frame of the documentary is recorded. An exhaustive check on diseases in the areas where we would be filming meant a thorough examination of our respective vaccination records. Rabies, malaria, tetanus, typhoid, and cholera were the main concerns. Where there was any doubt at all, we got jabs and boosters before we left the country. Then came the small matter of paying our way. Money is always a nightmare when you are shooting a film. Not so much getting the budget in the first place, but paying people as the filming progresses. Some of the more experienced fixers had established bank accounts and one could wire them money by electronic bank transfer. But how would we pay for the hire of transport and extra filming equipment in Banda Aceh? Half the bank buildings had been razed to the ground. Our local contact had indicated his preference for being paid cash, in US dollars. We'd also need money to tip people. All this meant the team having to take wads of hard currency with us (and avoiding the danger of memory lapses and placing it insecurely in the hold on board the plane).

Next item on the agenda: packing. Bad enough that our trip was scheduled to be five or six weeks long at least, but as an on-screen presenter, I had to give special consideration about what to wear. This was not going to be a shoot that required jackets and ties, for sure. But then, the dangers of looking too informal? In addition, the recurring nightmare of continuity; that situation in the film edit where you want to compress two scenes into one and the reporter somehow exits left frame wearing a green shirt and magically enters right frame wearing totally different clothes. I had learned from experience to buy several shirts and trousers of the same color and rotate them. Even then, I was aware of viewers asking you incessantly why you wore the "same clothes" every day on location and posing questions about hygiene! Naturally, sheer weight of luggage would play a big part in one's ultimate selection. I'd always preferred rucksacks to suitcases. They were lighter and the numerous zip compartments meant it was always easier to find documents, medication, sunglasses and hats in a hurry. There was no point in overpacking. Our small team would have more than a dozen items of recording equipment to lug all around South Asia. The last thing we needed was to be weighed down by unnecessary baggage brought about by stuffing endless clothes into our bags; clothes that might never see the light of day. Pack light and wash often was also a good principle in theory, but it rarely worked. In practice you were always on the move and never in one place long enough to get your clothes dry. I settled on a series of blue shirts, knee-length long shorts and lightweight pale grey trousers.

All of this preparation took a month or two. By the spring of 2005 we had done as much as we could to get ourselves ready. Our budget was just over three hundred thousand dollars. We had the usual tense discussions about travel options. Understandably, your production manager is concerned that the project comes in on budget. Reporting an overspend is a sure-fire way for an independent production company to get itself into a broadcaster's bad books with all the attendant consequences for future program commissions. It's one of the rare mortal sins in the world of television (the other is libeling a Hollywood celebrity and ending up with a three-million-dollar legal bill). So we had the inevitable airline route discussions. Yes, we know if you changed planes four times and had a seven-hour stopover in Doha you could shave five hundred dollars off each ticket, but did we really want a twenty-six-hour journey from London to Jakarta before we changed planes twice more? Would that really be the best preparation to getting our filming mission off to a relaxing and encouraging start?

After lengthy discussions, we compromised on a plan that would get us there. It wasn't the cheapest route, nor was it the most expensive. On April 30, 2005, Charlie Hawes, Bruno Sorrentino, and I met up at Terminal Three at London's Heathrow airport and divided up the bags in the best manner possible to avoid excess baggage costs. At check-in, I spelt out the nature of the film we were making to the airline staff and used every available charm technique to negotiate us a 50 percent discount. We took the gear with our international customs carnet to get the paperwork stamped before departure and headed off under the sign saying "Departures".

The next time I would see Heathrow would be six weeks from now.

I had no idea of what was about to unfold on my tsunami journey.

2

Banda Aceh

The Islamic Response

IF YOU ARE STARTING off from London, Western Sumatra in north-western Indonesia must be one of the trickiest places to get to in the world. You could make it to Togo or Fiji more speedily. As we awaited our connecting flights via Medan to Banda Aceh from Jakarta, the nation's capital, we were, at once, confronted with the practical consequences of our decision to travel without a specialist sound recordist. Our cameraman, Bruno Sorrentino, had been adamant that he could double up on both picture and sound. It would, of course, be more time consuming, but our production executives had persuaded us it would make huge cost savings on the budget. Flights, hotel bills, and wages overheads could all be struck off from the expenditure column. But as Bruno, producer Charlie Hawes, and I awaited our luggage at the baggage carousel before clearing immigration and customs, it dawned on us that when you are a team member down, the usually onerous task of retrieving about seventeen items of equipment and personal belongings suddenly went from being a chore to being a daunting physical challenge. We had secured three luggage carts, one each. But as all the silver boxes mounted up, as best as we tried, we just couldn't get everything onto the three trolleys. Bruno was already laden down with the camera (he had had this on board the plane. Cameramen *never* put their cameras down in the hold, despite all the best efforts of the world's airline staff to persuade them to part company with them. It is practically a marriage. They are joined at the hip). So, it ended up with Charlie scurrying to find a fourth trolley and we then took it in turns to slalom through the airport pushing one cart ahead and pulling another behind with all the gear wobbling precariously as we inched our way forward. All this after eighteen hours of travel, horrendous jet lag, and an airport concourse absolutely jammed with people. Television often appears to the outside world as a glamorous profession. Yet so often this could not be further from the truth.

Two more short flights and, finally, we were approaching Banda Aceh at the northern tip of western Sumatra, precisely 5.54 degrees north of the equator. As our aircraft descended through the thick clouds, we craned our necks to try and see through the tiny windows out to the emerging land below. So much was flattened. As far as the eye could see, kilometers and kilometers of houses had been razed to the ground as though some monumental bulldozer had been let loose and had mercilessly claimed all before it. My mind flitted back to my father and that December 26 BBC news report: *"God could have stopped that."*

At least on arrival we received some welcome assistance with those hefty cases. Our location producer, Fauzan, came to meet us in a large white van. "How old is he?" I asked Charlie, discreetly. "I mean, he looks straight out of high school." Indeed, this fresh-faced eager beaver had barely turned twenty years of age. He had been recommended to us after work he had carried out with a series of international news organizations in the weeks following the initial disaster.

Our trip from the airport took us through rickety shanty towns. Kids played unselfconsciously on the streets in tatty clothes as mangy dogs stared up pitifully at our passing vehicle. Miraculously some of the buildings still appeared to be intact. One of these was to be our base for the next eight days, the Aceh Hotel. This was practically the only remaining hostel that could accommodate the motley crews of journalists, NGO employees, and relief workers. As we arrived at reception with our mountain of boxes and bags, Fauzan turned to us and said, "This place is about two thirds full. The rooms are on five floors, so the guy at reception wants to know which floor you all want to stay on." Bruno, Charlie, and I all exchanged looks. One word came immediately into my mind. Aftershocks. What if, months after the calamitous earthquake, there were more earth tremors? The foundations and walls of many of these buildings had already been weakened. It wouldn't take much to topple them. Questions. Would it be safer to be on the ground floor, nearer the exit for a hasty escape? Or would your room end up at the bottom of a heap of rubble? Better, perhaps, on the top floor, then you would have very little falling on you? (OK, the ceiling and roof of the building, that, I grant you, but rather smaller fare in comparison.) On the other hand, from the top floor, if everything collapsed, you would go hurtling down five stories to the bottom. Maybe it was time for the Aristotelian mean? Maybe the middle floor was the best option? After a lengthy deliberation in the heart of the hotel foyer we concluded that, frankly, nowhere would be safe if there was a sizeable aftershock. There were already gaping fissures up and down the walls with gaps measuring several centimeters in the plaster. There was an elevator, and by all accounts, it was actually working. But the received wisdom was that it would be unwise to use it just in case there was a sudden tremor and it came to a halt between floors. After much discussion, we plumped for the top floor. A porter grabbed my blue rucksack and one of the boxes of equipment and gestured to me to follow him. Up the winding stairs and finally, at the top, he showed me to my fifth-floor room. The first thing I noticed after I opened the door was a large emerald-green arrow positioned carefully to the right of the window, at a forty-five-degree angle to the window frame. "Is that pointing towards the emergency exit?" I asked in very slow, deliberate English. A puzzled look. Then the porter pointed to the arrow, pulled up a small rug at the foot of the bed and affected to pray. Immediately I got it. It was the *qibla*, a directional aid for Muslims so that they could align their prayer mats and orient themselves towards the *Kaaba* at the sacred mosque in Mecca. Emergency exit? So much for my inter-faith credentials and weeks of intensive research in the British Library. Such was my anxiety after all the talk of aftershocks that all I could think of was the quickest escape route out of the room.

My porter had been really helpful. I had no idea what was now expected from me (in a New York hotel it would have been a ten-dollar tip at the very least). But I had no local currency. All I had was an uneaten chocolate bar stuffed into my jacket pocket, hastily stored away from the plane flight between Medan and Aceh. I plunged my hand into my coat and produced it with a flourish. "It's all I have for you at the moment," I said. A huge beam broke out across the assistant's face. "Many many weeks now I not have these things," he replied. He took it and bade me farewell. I had left the door slightly ajar and seconds later I could hear the wrapper being hastily removed outside in the corridor. Gentle, hurried scoffing of an Indonesian Kit-Kat ensued.

I now collapsed on my bed for what I thought would be forty winks. Then, without the slightest warning, a deafening noise burst through the open window. I leapt up and craned my neck to see the mosque's main entrance situated a mere thirty meters away. People were filing in for *maghrib*, the fourth session of five in the cycle of daily prayer. Although this differs from country to country, it is traditionally practiced around sunset. For the next nine days, I got used to the vocal prowess and power of the muezzin, as his call to prayer, the *salat*, punctuated the day. The bad news for poor old jet-lagged me was that the first of these sessions, the *fajr*, dawn prayer, began typically around just after 4.30 every morning. I did think for a minute or two about asking reception for another room but thought better of it. First day in a totally new place and I'd effectively be telling the hotel staff that I wasn't too keen on their centuries-old religious customs. No. Wax earplugs would have to do. For all that the countries of the Middle East dominate the western news agenda, it is Indonesia which is the country with the largest Muslim population in the world. Of its two hundred and twenty-five million citizens, nearly 90 percent identify as followers of the prophet Muhammed and the Qur'an. In Aceh, this figure rises to a staggering 98 percent, and its title, "Serambi Mekkah", meaning "Mecca's Verandah", gives an idea of its geopolitical significance. Six thousand two hundred kilometers of Indian Ocean separate this north-western tip of Indonesia from the most sacred and revered site in Islam. The seventh century revelations to the Prophet came to these parts some six hundred years later, largely through Arab traders. By 1292, Marco Polo, on his return from China, witnessed the establishment of several Muslim towns in the region.

After a fitful first night's sleep, dramatically curtailed by the dawn efforts of the muezzin, we set off for our first day of filming in the direction of Sigli, some seventy miles east along the coast. Here, we were due to meet with a young man, Fadil Bania Arifin. Our fixer, Fauzan, briefed me on the way there about his back story. On the fateful day of the tsunami, Fadil had just celebrated his brother's marriage and had been surrounded by family members. Some six hundred guests had been in attendance, and it had been his job to get all the marquees back to the suppliers after hours and hours of wedding celebrations.

"How many family members did he lose then?" I asked Fauzan.

"All of them," came the reply. "He's the sole remaining member. About twenty or more relatives died I think." Charlie and I exchanged looks. Silence. At that point, our van passed a most extraordinary sight. A huge wooden boat resting on top of a house. The vessel had been swept along by the wave and had come to rest on the roof of the building as the waters had subsided. Our vehicle screeched to a halt and out came the camera. This would happen every day for the next week or more. Image after image. Some disturbing, others just plain bizarre, as though the world was obeying a completely different set of laws of physics. After two hours or more, we trundled into Sigli. Fadil was waiting for us, pacing around nervously. He was a slim, wiry man in his mid-twenties with huge, sad brown eyes. He tried a smile as we shook hands, but it soon petered out into cracks around the edges. On December 26, 2004, he had tried to cram as many of his family members into his small blue pickup truck to escape the terror of the advancing wave. We went with him to the local mosque which turned out to be a hugely significant location in the events of that day. As the vehicle pulled alongside the building with some dozen or more human beings holding on, the water had suddenly swept Fadil out of his van and directly into the mosque. "And then I saw my sister in front of me," he told me. "She was hanging on with her daughter in her hands. All she had was a cable, like a telephone cable. Then when I next looked, her daughter was gone. Then, my sister . . . she let go of the cable." His eyes welled up. So did mine. He took me into the mosque and showed me round. Everywhere there were battered, half-intact copies of the Qur'an. Most of them had been totally doused in water and been left for weeks to dry out. Pages were crumpled up, but the unmistakable Arabic text was as sharp and focused as ever. The supporting columns inside the mosque were buckled yet somehow still supporting the roof. Fadil explained that as the water surged in, it had blown out the windows, allowing the levels to finally subside just as he thought he might drown. Then, clambering to safety after his near-death ordeal he had apprehensively wandered back to the blue van outside. As he opened the passenger door, he saw two bodies: his mother and, tightly wrapped in her arms, a tiny child, one of Fadil's many young nephews. For a moment, I just forgot this was a TV interview and had to place my arm around him. It was only a few weeks since I had had to identify my own father in that funeral parlor. But to lose a parent in such traumatic circumstances was truly shocking. After we had covered all the details of what had happened that day, I now really wanted to talk to Fadil about his faith in God. Was he angry with Allah after all that had happened? "I am not angry with my God," he told me. "If God has taken away my family, then maybe it just means it is time for my family to die." Why would God, I asked, allow this to happen to him? "It is a test, a test of my faith," he said to me resolutely.

"Is your faith now weaker or stronger after what happened with the tsunami?" I asked him. He fixed his gaze on me.

"Stronger," he replied. He got up, found an unfinished cigarette in his trouser-pocket, and peeled away from us to a quiet side alley for a restorative drag and a few moments of balm offered by solitude.

I spent hours with Fadil, on and off camera, and not once in all my time with him was there a remote sense of self-pity, the understandable "why me?" response that puts the individual at the center of the events. I have never really got the "why me?" thing anyhow. My private response, unuttered, of course, has nearly always been, "well, why not?" I'm in good company here. American President Joe Biden is no stranger to misfortune having lost his wife, Neilia, and young daughter, Naomi, in a car accident and, much later on, his forty-six-year-old son, Beau, to brain cancer. Above his desk he keeps a framed cartoon by the artist Dik Browne. It depicts the red-bearded Viking warrior, Hagar the Horrible. As his vessel is struck by a storm and in the process of sinking, he looks up to the heavens. "Why me?" he enquires angrily. "Why not?" comes the reply. There was a sense of resignation to Fadil and that if Allah did have purposes and motives in events like the 2004 tsunami, then they were ultimately unknowable. But was his take on all this representative of the wider culture? He had, after all, been the first person I had engaged on the subject.

After farewells, hugs, and promises to post on to him a Manchester United soccer scarf on my return to the United Kingdom, we said our goodbyes to Fadil. His meager frame grew smaller and smaller as our vehicle pulled away from the mosque where we left him. A man, now utterly alone in the world save for his girlfriend, the one member of his inner circle who had been spared the destructive wave's brutal impact.

The logistics of journeying in our modest white van was a daily nightmare. Road bridges throughout the area had been destroyed back in December which meant that any trip "as the crow flies" became an impossibility. In our hotel foyer, teams of journalists and international relief workers pored over makeshift maps and exchanged navigational intelligence on how best to get from A to B. At times, the only advisable route to one's desired destination was the equivalent of driving from Washington to New York via a lengthy detour through Pittsburgh. We listened carefully to what people were saying and, if necessary, adjusted our plans. Sometimes it would entail a lengthy diversion adding an hour or two to our time on the road. Often that meant a six in the morning start instead of eight o'clock.

Grabbing whatever food was around at that time in the hotel for breakfast was essential. There would be nothing more to eat for hours. We survived on a very large box of bananas and bottled water.

My next encounter was of a totally different nature from Fadil's heart-breaking tale. I was off to meet a Muslim academic with whom I could really get to grips with this whole question of God and the suffering of his human subjects. Professor Yusny Saby taught Islamic philosophy at Banda Aceh University. He was waiting, patiently, for the crew in his classroom and my immediate impressions were hugely positive. A friendly, animated man in his mid-fifties perhaps, wearing a black *songkuk*, an Indonesian version of the Arabian fez which had, no doubt, been introduced by those traders from the Middle East all those centuries ago. The camera lights gave off glints from his very large spectacles as we took to our task. It was not long before the "T" word came into play, a word that Fadil had cited with great regularity.

"Anybody in the world, whether you are a pious man or a crooked man, can be tested," assured Dr Saby. "Men should be stronger and closer to God, when tested, if they pass. If they don't pass, they may be further away from God. Because of this tragedy, they may even blame God. You are not just if you do that."

I was not at all happy with this notion of an eternal creator who took on the guise of some supernatural driving instructor: pass/fail. But this academic, with thirty years or more of teaching experience assured me that Allah was not some uncaring tyrant. In doing so, he pointed up a well-known verse from the Qur'an: "On no soul doth Allah place a burden greater than it can bear."[1] But surely there were cases, many times, when individuals are stretched to breaking point and beyond? At such points they despair, give in and yes, *in extremis*, they can even take their own lives. I let this pass and listened on.

The learned scholar was now in full stride and quite energized. At one point his black felt *songkok* actually slipped from his head as he quoted another relevant Qur'anic citation. "There are among men some who serve Allah, as it were, on the verge: if good befalls them, they are, therewith, well content; but if a trial comes to them, they turn on their faces: they lose both this world and the Hereafter: that is loss for all to see!"[2] Moreover, Dr Saby was swift to pour scorn on any neat relationship between virtue being

1. Holy Qur'an, Sūrah 2 Al-Baqarah v 286.
2. Holy Qur'an, Sūrah 22 Al-Hajj v 11.

automatically rewarded with prosperity in the earthly realm and wickedness attracting divine wrath and punishment. "Humans are tested whether they are good or not, there is no escape from trials and tribulations. As the Qur'an makes clear, faith is not an insurance policy against misfortune," he insisted. Another extract from the Holy Book. "Do men believe that they will be left alone on saying, 'We believe' and that they will not be tested?"[3] These words were a long way from the agonizing and hand-wringing characterized by many Christian commentators after the tsunami. There was a muscularity and frank willingness to admit to the question of human suffering that lay beyond the mind's comprehension. I had one last go and asked Dr Saby why God would permit the death of so many thousands of people in Aceh and nearby because of an agenda based on testing his subjects. Surely this was just too high a price to pay and brought belief in Allah into ridicule?

"This of course, is a difficult question," he said to me, at last sounding less than certain of himself. "What is in the mind of God? We cannot know that. What is there in the wisdom of God? We just cannot know."

"Have you," I asked him, "ever doubted the existence of God?" A long pause accompanied by a furrowed brow.

"What do you mean by that?" he asked. Maybe in this part of the world, it was the first time he had ever heard the question put.

"That maybe, God is a creation of the human mind and imagination?" I responded. An even further tightening of the furrowed brow.

"No, I have never thought that" he said, looking at me with not a little pity and incredulity.

There are more than ninety-nine names given to God in Qur'anic references. There is no suggestion of polytheism here. God's oneness, captured by the Arabic term *tawheed*, attests to the Deity's indivisibility. The name Allah, of course, takes pride of place, but the other names cited in Islam's Holy Book do not replace "Allah" but rather lay claim to his many qualities. In spite of numerous references to compassion and mercy, it is striking how many of these labels for the divine revolve around power and inscrutability. God is *al-aziz*, the Mighty, *al-wasi*, the Vast, and also *al-qahhaar*, and *al-baatin,* the Subduer and the Hidden. This for me was a long cry from repetitive exhortations from my childhood about the baby Jesus in the manger and mantras from the clergy and religious brothers whose steady and persistent assurance was that "God is Love".

3. Holy Qur'an, Sūrah 29 Al-'Ankabūut v 2.

Some hours later, reflecting on the encounter with Dr Saby, my mind turned to one of the Old Testament's most celebrated characters—the hapless figure of Job. Here was a man, much like Fadil, the young man who had lost more than twenty family members to the tsunami. Job was a biblical figure of decency and good public standing who suffered calamity after calamity. His infamous comforters fall into the trap of insisting Job must have sinned greatly because the only explanation for such misfortunes is divine punishment. And the story ends with Job none the wiser. In the denouement, he asks God to explain himself. Why has he, an upright and loyal man, had to endure such affliction? God answers back in unambiguous fashion. "Where were you when I laid the foundation of the earth? Tell me if you have understanding. Who determined its measurements—surely you know!"[4] For two whole chapters Yahweh questions the pitiful Job. Is it by human wisdom that the hawk soars, or the mountains rise above the sea? Has Job commanded the dawn or comprehended the expanse of the earth? At the end of the tirade, Job has no option but to concede defeat. "See, I am of small account; what shall I answer you? I lay my hand on my mouth. I have spoken once, and I will not answer; twice, but will proceed no further."[5]

The Book of Job is hugely significant in the history of theodicy. As long as two and a half thousand years ago it decisively broke any simple link that says prosperity is due reward for following God's statutes and that trials are the inevitable outcome for those that disobey. No. The wicked on earth can, and do, prosper. The virtuous are visited with setbacks and undeserved suffering. Why does God allow this? This biblical tale echoes the Islamic take, namely that God's ways are beyond human comprehension. As Dr Saby told me, we cannot know. Of course, in a world of one and half billion Muslims, it would be surprising if there was not some dissent and questioning of these largely consensual understandings. Aceh in Indonesia is 99 percent Sunni but in Iran, with its majority Shia population, one finds strains of the questioning and anger with God that echoes not only the Psalms, but also modern Christian theodicies. In southern Iran in 2003 (coincidentally also on Boxing Day like the Indian Ocean tsunami a year later), after the earthquake in Bam which accounted for more than twenty-six thousand lives, an anguished poet penned the following:

4. Job 38:4–5.
5. Job 40:4–5.

As the ceilings tumbled, when dust filled the eyes and mouths
Struts and beams landed on heads and necks
Did he not see babies sucking on their mothers' breasts?
Did he not see shy new brides climbing into their nuptial beds?
Did he not see flocks of faithful in nocturnal prayers?
Did he not see feverish bodies dreaming of good health?
Did he not see? Did he not? Did he?
Would you keep on saying "my God is kind?"
Would you, for the sake of your kind God, define kindness for me?[6]

Powerful words indeed. Yet in Aceh, it was proving almost impossible to locate anyone who remotely echoed this sentiment of outrage, of doubt. And this in a part of the world that had lost more than a hundred thousand lives since the fateful events of December 26. We were now three days into our week-long stay in Sumatra, and at the end of a long Saturday's filming, our commendably organized and energetic location fixer pulled a rather surprising rabbit out of the hat. "You know that there's a Catholic Church here in Aceh?" he said, as though I might have had it highlighted in bold red ink in my Lonely Planet Guide.

"What?" I retorted. "How can that be? It's 99.9 percent Muslim and they operate a regime of Sharia law." A phone call or two later and we had arranged with the local priest to go and film the following morning at Sunday mass.

Father Fernando Severi greeted us in the sacristy of the Church of the Sacred Heart. What a character. He was like something out of a Graham Greene novel. A tall man with a very healthy mane of longish gray hair, he strutted around his church like a peacock, pointing out instructions to his parishioners about where hymn books should be placed. He marshalled a small group of altar boys like a border collie rounding up sheep and gestured to us to take our places in a pew near the front of the church. This striking Italian figure had devoted some thirty-eight years of his priestly vocation to service in Indonesia. He had a modicum of workmanlike English, but providentially, we had a bilingual cameraman, so planning continued in fluent Italian. Another linguistic jump, as mass was conducted in the local language, but as every Catholic will tell you, the structure of the liturgy is the same the world over and it was easy to follow what was going on even if I was totally lost during his homily. So far from home and in such strange surroundings, it felt good to be back in a eucharistic service once more.

6. Esfahani, *Keep On Saying*.

Following mass, we were offered coffee and we set up to carry out the interview in a room just off the sacristy. Father Fernando was wearing a rather jazzy blue and black shirt, more akin to a late fifties rock 'n' roll star than a member of the clergy. When I kicked off the interview by asking him if the tsunami had prompted him to have doubts about God and his intentions, he was immediately on the front foot.

"I understand your question and the intention behind it," he said animatedly. "But are you really asking me, a priest charged with teaching others about the central notion of suffering and death in the Christian faith, if I have doubts? Really, this could be seen as an insult to our—to my faith. For we Christians know that our salvation lies through the cross."

That certainly put me in my place. It seemed that some of the local Islamic muscularity had rubbed off on this particular cleric. Not the slightest hint of a wobble, in spite of being surrounded by months of carnage. So, I wanted to know, what did he make of the local faith response to the adverse events? Compared with so many Christians who had raised their doubts, was he not impressed with the resolute stance taken by people like Fadil, Dr Saby, and others who steadfastly refused to put God in the dock? His answer was forthright, if perhaps lacking in inter-faith political correctness. And for some unexplained reason, he now broke off from his native Italian and gave me his answer in English.

"I admire their faith. But the value of this faith is diminished by the fact that they have reached this statement, not through their own experience or choice. They have received this statement from the Muslim authorities, and they just repeat it."

Really? Was Fadil's earlier conviction that his faith in Allah was now stronger than before, largely due to him following the party line and spouting what the authorities told him? In a week, I wasn't going to be able to conduct a huge opinion poll among the Achinese population, nor interview more than a dozen or so people, but my impressions weren't just formed by our formal interviews. En route to locations, we had spent hours talking with Fauzan and meeting a lot of his associates. I can honestly say that they were, at best, bemused by the premise of my journalistic and religious enquiry. They were, of course, polite, and the dynamics were perhaps complicated by the fact that we were in a client–provider relationship. But I did detect, more than once, looks of incredulity on many faces. Question God, his goodness, nay his very *existence*? What a strange response! Who were these weak-willed Christians from far flung shores?

When I took my leave of Father Fernando, I was more than a tad concerned. One recurring theme in one's journeys as an enquiring journalist was the small matter of the fallout from documentaries. It is all very well for people to open up on location and for them to tell it from the heart. But you get to fly back to London with all the footage and weeks, months later, once it hits the air, there can often be repercussions on the ground for the people left behind. Here was a lone Catholic priest in the middle of a huge Islamic sea, often dominated by hard men with ambitions. In such contexts, the vortex of religious ideas and political agendas could easily become twisted. There are often casualties. I raised these anxieties with Charlie and Bruno, but their response was one and the same: he's been here thirty-eight years, he's well-established, and he knows the fine line between what he can say and not say. In the end, he was such an uncompromising and principled individual, perhaps he didn't care. He had spoken his truth.

I was to come face to face with one of those "hard men with ambitions" only the following day. The Islamic Defenders Front, or Front Pembela Islam (FPI) in local vernacular, was founded in 1998 with a view to campaigning for the reintroduction of Sharia law. This they achieved in Aceh in 2001. Movies, karaoke, and outward displays of affection between unmarried persons are punishable by floggings outside mosques, actions which are carried out in front of huge crowds and then shared online. This is a society where, for survival's sake, you rein in your impulses. The minute you walk out your front door, everything is on show. In this goldfish bowl of hypervigilance, you make every effort to conform.

The FPI's designated spokesman in the area was a man with every appearance of being a "young turk": Yusuf Al-Qarhawy. To get to him we had to muscle our way past a group of young minders on the door of a drab municipal building. When we found him, he was sitting cross-legged on the stone floor, dressed in a red and white Arabian *kaffiyah* or headdress. He reminded me of a young Yasser Arafat. I extended my hand, but my gesture of physical contact was politely spurned. The lights were very dim. There were minders leaning against the walls. Not a woman in sight. So, how did the Islamic Defenders account for the devastating events of a few months back? It was not quite the answer I was expecting.

"Islam forbids people to wear tight clothes. It forbids young people to go off to quiet places on their own, going off on motorbikes with someone who is not your husband," opined Yusuf. "It's well known that all sorts of things go on. Like on the beach at Lampu. Things that are prohibited by Allah. So, all this had to be cleansed."

What a strangely uncompassionate God this Allah must be, I thought, if he was prepared to sacrifice thousands of innocent beings, many of them children, just to get back at the handful of offenders who were wearing spray-on jeans and surrendering a little too readily to their biological urges. I put it to him that his reaction was just a case of doing what religious zealots had done since time immemorial, namely the opportunistic use of natural disasters to exert social and political control of a population. He was having none of it. "No, no. We don't force people, we just invite them," he said with sinister understatement. "They have to reflect on the fact that what has hit them is a lesson, so that we don't do it all again." He could have said that the people were simply unlucky in being in the wrong place at the wrong time. He could have said that the local population should have heeded warning signs from local wildlife which had sensed powerful rumblings underfoot minutes before the tsunami struck and scarpered hotfoot into the local hills in pursuit of higher ground. But no. It was a message aimed at the local youthful population: do not imitate western fashion and sexual mores. If you do, then God will awake from his slumber and drown thousands of people, 99.9 percent of whom had nothing to do with the offending behavior in question. If this rationalization is all that it is on offer, then sign me up without further ado for the Richard Dawkins' fan club.

Whatever one's understanding of the Dawkins position, I was, of course, hugely admiring of his work as a scientist, especially his 1976 work *The Selfish Gene,* a book which in a recent survey even trumped Charles Darwin's *Origin of Species* as the most influential science book of all time.[7] What, I wondered, would an Islamic scientist make of my God and natural disasters faith dilemma? In particular, what would a Muslim geologist make of tectonic plates and the manner in which planet earth had been fashioned? I asked Fauzan to find me someone to speak to. Ever resourceful on a mobile phone that was eternally in use, and which never seemed to run down its battery, he proudly announced he had pulled another rabbit out of the hat.

And so it was next day that we met Didik Sugyanto, a young geologist. We needed, somehow, to concoct a way of demonstrating for a television

7. https://royalsociety.org/news/2017/07/science-book-prize-poll-results/#:~:text=Richard%20Dawkins'%201976%20book%2C%20The,Royal%20Society%20Science%20Book%20Prize.

audience the phenomenon of tectonic plates. There are seven major plates in the earth's crust, or lithosphere to give it its more technical name. At our beachside location, we set about gathering up a series of large stones or small rocks with flat surfaces which would, jigsaw-style, fit together reasonably well. This would give the viewer some representation of the plates, each of which are around a hundred kilometers thick and reach temperatures of anywhere between two hundred and four hundred degrees centigrade. "This is the mantle, where magma activities take place," Didik explained, lifting up the stones and pointing to the bed beneath supporting each of the "plates". "And here is the earth's crust. It is thin, made up of plates, and plastic in nature. Some plates when they meet only rub against one another, but it gets very dangerous when there's penetration of the plates. This is called subduction, and that's when you get earthquakes." I was a total ignoramus about all this stuff. My excuse was that I had dropped geography aged thirteen and never got beyond the basics of simple river valleys.

After ten minutes or so assembling and reassembling the various stones or "plates" and having established the geological facts, we shifted gear. I wanted to know, as a Muslim scientist, how Didik coped with the design question. Had Allah created a faulty model? Because if you live in Turkey, California, Lisbon or anywhere on planet earth close to the fault lines of these structures, your life was always going to be under threat from a once in a lifetime mega earth tremor. "Muslims believe that God has made the world as it is in accordance with the needs of the human race," he said confidently. "Of course, these disasters have already been mentioned in our Holy Book."

"Yes, I know about the Qur'anic references," I told him. "But I am asking you as a geologist. Can planet earth work for humans, without there being these horribly dangerous tectonic plates?"

He looked at me quizzically. Maybe it was because he wasn't used to hypothetical questions? He thought long and hard, took a deep breath and answered me again. "God has designed the world for human beings in such a way so that we learn, study, and work hard. It's not easy, it's a challenge. God hasn't made the world in order to spoil us.

"As it is said in the Holy Book, whatever happens in the end, the apocalypse will come," he insisted, rather unnervingly. "However, God protects the sustainability of the planet through regeneration. The old will be replaced by the new. The planet isn't static. If it was static there'd be decay, and the apocalypse would be upon us immediately." I did try three, four times to have him address the Leibniz formula, whether this was indeed the "best of all possible worlds", but each time, in answer to my question, I got an answer that simply described the world *as it was*. And maybe I was wrong here, but it seemed to me that I was somehow being ungrateful or irreverent in even raising the question of whether God had somehow done less than a satisfactory job. At one point in the filming, at the third or fourth unsatisfactory answer, I even turned away from Didik and looked straight into the camera, to the viewer, if you will, with a look of frustrated exasperation. Yet, not for the first or last time in my life, in retrospect, I was not listening carefully: a cardinal error for a journalist. *The old will be replaced by the new. The planet isn't static.* There was much in this insight which I should have picked up on. I should have encouraged Didik to unpack this and develop his point. This theme of the interdependency of creative and destructive forces was to assume great significance further down the road of exploration. It is, frankly, embarrassing for me to look back on this now and conclude that I was not paying my interviewee the attention he merited. It was a lost opportunity. I had been grandstanding in front of the camera. I now blush every time I see this exchange. But it is too late.

It was now getting on for nearly a week since we arrived in Sumatra, though it seemed more like a month. These had been long, intense days. We had eaten sporadically, were probably mildly dehydrated and possibly in danger of ignoring our physical condition and living off sheer adrenalin. Each day brought new scenes of destruction. One hastily constructed shanty town heralded visitors with a sign inscribed on cardboard on corrugated iron. It read: "Tsunami City: Welcome to Hell." Day after day of this was beginning to corrode my spirits—and I was lucky: I had an exit pass back to a first world home. London was not, as far as I was aware, located on a tectonic plate fault line. After our session with the geologist, I spoke to our team about something which had been bothering me for a day or two. This projected documentary we were hoping to air in the UK and around the world would be of substantial duration, about one hundred minutes in all. In such a film, you needed light and shade, changes of gear, surprises. No one, but no one, would be able to tune into a hundred minutes of grief, anger, and destruction. My argument was even more compelling when we realized that Channel Four UK was proposing to transmit this on—wait for it—Christmas Day in the evening. Just at the time when the family is full of turkey, Christmas pudding, and has pulled crackers, our team would have them nestle down on the sofa to nearly two hours of what might appear a glimpse of Armageddon. We needed some hope, something positive, some *deus ex machina* to lift our sagging spirits. Then, out of the blue, came deliverance. Our attention was drawn to a series of yellow posters dotted around a central square off one of Banda Aceh's busiest streets. There was a face on them which, the nearer we drew closer to them, came bizarrely into focus. "I don't believe it," I exclaimed. "I simply don't believe it." As we came up close against one of the posters which was fluttering in the early morning breeze, I observed the image of Portuguese Manchester United soccer forward, Cristiano Ronaldo, staring directly at me. Now I am a huge United fan and for a moment, I had to pinch myself. Was I dreaming?

"Fauzan," I said to our location producer, "what does all this text say at the foot of this poster?" He squinted and took in all the writing.

"It says that this guy is coming here tomorrow on a charity mission, to donate money to children and knock a soccer ball around with them." My faith in God had been miraculously restored in a flash. Ronaldo, in 2005, was not quite the international superstar he is now. In the contemporary soccer world he is a supreme athlete, having won more than thirty major trophies and the celebrated *Balon d'Or* best world soccer player award five times. Back in 2004 after the wave hit Aceh, he was said to have been moved by the image in the press of a youngster named Martunis. The young kid had been playing football wearing a Portuguese soccer shirt on the beach when the wave hit the shores of Banda Aceh. Press reports said he only survived because he had clung to a tree for days on end and then survived on fragments of dried noodles in the aftermath. So inspired and moved by the image of this boy wearing his national soccer shirt, Ronaldo was now flying out to make his own contribution.

The following day, the crowds gathered on this open ground just outside the center of Aceh. Thousands of young survivors, many of them orphans, were waving pennants and staring up to the skies. A helicopter was circling above and closing in. Huge expectation. I looked at Bruno our cameraman. "How are they going to manage this?" I asked him. "There's loads of people here, but no area cordoned off for him." Dozens of military personnel were on hand, but they weren't doing much to segregate the crowds. The chopper landed some distance away and Ronaldo was escorted the remainder of the short journey by bus. But once he descended, it all deteriorated into total chaos. He carried a soccer ball under his arm and walked onto the huge grassy area ahead of us. Two or three very nervous-looking security guards accompanied him, but they were powerless as a surge of onlookers totally surrounded them. Poor old Bruno was in the thick of the scrum, trying to get pictures and fighting off the masses. There was nothing set up: no secured space for the soccer player, no podium, no microphones. Ronaldo's security guards were now getting really edgy, and it was no surprise when, after two or three minutes of this mayhem, they pulled the plug on the event. The footballer was led back to the bus to pose for some media photos alongside Martunis and then off he sped. I looked around at the kids' faces. Enormous anti-climax. All this had been inspired by my desire to find something upbeat to include in our portrayal of the current mood in Aceh but it had backfired somewhat. Those children. What future for them?

After a brief break, the youth theme continued with our next filming location. Fauzan had lined up a visit to an orphanage. This was something he had been working on for some time and I had not been especially looking forward to it. More than one hundred and sixty young boys, most of them without mother, father, aunts, and uncles to care for them. As we arrived, they were all at work—drawing. It was a session of art therapy, as one of the tutors explained to us:

"I say to them, draw anything you like, and they use two principal colors, red and black. I ask them 'why those colors?' And they answer, it's blood mixed with tsunami water." I took the opportunity to wander around and admire the artwork with my own eyes. There was a surprising similarity to a lot of the creative designs. Almost every effort contained mosques and mountains.

"Why so?" I asked one of their teachers.

"They were the only structures left after the tsunami struck," came the reply. These children had been through so much and their tutors were very sensitive about not disrupting and disturbing them too much. I asked if we could speak to one of them, gently.

The teachers all looked at one another and nodded. "Shukrullah," they said. "He's the one for you. Very tough and together. He'll be OK." We filmed them at prayer. All in line, all bowing and moving together in unison. It gave them solidarity, belonging and a sense of family cohesion. "Even if I am wrong and there isn't a God," I thought to myself, "this faith has given these traumatized children a sense of togetherness." It was possibly the difference between staying sane and losing your mind.

We were then introduced to Shukrullah. A serious-looking, well-built boy of about eight or nine years with an impish face. He wore a neat-fitting black felt *songkuk* hat which was quite elaborately adorned with a gold patterned rim. "I lost all my family," he told me. "After the tsunami happened there were times when I was on my own when I would cry. I cried because of my past. I remember my sins. Too many." Sins? This was an eight-year-old addressing me. He went on. "And I know that judgment day is closing in. It is like a test from Allah. Because we have done many sinful things, and so we are tested. It's up to us if the tsunami changes our lives or not."

Test. The "T" word again. Fadil had used it. Dr Saby had repeated it and now here was an eight-year-old consolidating the message. I so wanted to empathize with them after all they had been through, but I was repelled by such an understanding of Godhead. It set the world up as some sort of army camp with us all having to duck and weave, avoiding obstacles and having to endure setback after setback. If any parent had boobytrapped the nursery with barbed wire amidst all the cuddly toys, we'd rightfully be hauling them off in front of the courts. I shook hands with little Shukrullah and he looked me in the eye in a determined fashion. He was, indeed, a true survivor.

We were now a day or two away from having to draw a close to our time in Aceh and it was at that stage that, as a team, we had to look back at what we had achieved and decide how best to use the remainder of our time. Bruno, on camera, flagged up a couple of his own priorities.

He pointed out that so far, we had been unable to capture the huge extent of the flattened buildings as we had always been at ground level. Some of the news organizations had co-operated with NGOs and relief bodies and shared costs to charter a helicopter and get some arresting aerial views. But the kind of money they had was way beyond our budget. "Let's see if we can find a crane with a platform," said Bruno. So, our superbly well-connected local producer, Fauzan, immediately set to work. After half an hour on the mobile phone he claimed to have sorted it.

The following morning, we met the vehicle. We had been hoping that the driver would turn up with a stable platform attached to the vehicle, what we call in the trade a "cherry picker". This would allow Bruno to place his camera on a tripod and stabilize the recording equipment. Alas, when our crane pitched up in the midst of a desolate landscape of rubble, it came with a metal box suspended by a solid metallic chain. It looked secure and safe enough, but a worrying problem now presented itself. As the crane took us up high into the air, the fact that we were suspended by this huge rusty chain meant that the box we were in would simply revolve, non-stop. It would be impossible to get a steady shot as the box wasn't fixed to a platform or stable structure of any description. "Not to worry," said the ever-resourceful Bruno, "we'll just use that to our advantage. As long as the movement is smooth and not juddery, it'll look as though I am just gently panning with the camera." I was so pleased we had chosen Bruno for this shoot. This is precisely the pragmatic, can-do attitude you need on location when things are chopping and changing all the time and things don't always go according to plan. To have found a crane with a driver free at twenty hours' notice in Aceh was, in itself, a minor miracle. The last thing we needed, at this point in time, was a prima donna on camera complaining about the lack of a cherry-picker.

If you suffer from vertigo, a career in film or TV is probably not for you. The next thing we knew, we were about a hundred feet up in the air, absorbing a bird's eye view of a landscape that is just how I imagined Hiroshima must have looked in August 1945. For a couple of minutes, the two of us just fell silent. Then Bruno came out with a suggestion. "This is such a stunning backdrop," he said enthusiastically. "We should open the whole program with a long, developing shot that starts low down and as the panorama comes into shot, the viewer just sees for mile and miles what the tsunami has done." I agreed wholeheartedly. So, I set about composing an opening "piece to camera". These were the words that eventually made it into the opening minute of our transmitted documentary film:

"It's the biggest obstacle to religious belief, a question that has dogged mankind for centuries, how to reconcile natural disasters with belief in a loving and all-powerful creator. Tonight, as we remember the thousands of victims of the Asian tsunami, has God himself become the ultimate casualty?"

On the closing words, Bruno gently took the camera off me and carried on panning away to reveal the thousands of destroyed houses and public buildings. A solitary mosque remained standing far, far away on the horizon. After the crane lowered our metal box carefully back to the ground, we started to meander around the rubble. Haunting image after haunting image captured our attention. The most arresting of all was a solitary baby buggy with a mangled teddy bear inside it. It stood in eerie isolation amidst the ruins of an old house. Further afield, I spotted a lone child sitting on some crumbling steps. It was all that remained of what I presumed to be his former home. The youngster looked around. He resembled a compass whose needle had been spinning round incessantly in search of an elusive north.

After a much-needed break, Bruno took me to one side.

"I've an idea," he said. "Do we have anything particularly planned for the next two or three hours?" I turned to Charlie and Fauzan to enquire. They shook their heads.

"Nothing," I said to Bruno. "Why? What did you have in mind?"

"I'd like to do something a bit different," he said. "Let's just go and get an open back truck and put you on it and go for a ride. Staying around here would be fine. There's still so much to film."

Go for a ride? Behind Bruno's thinking was that so much of our filming to date had been planned. This especially extended to quite a few of my own contributions to camera. Being meticulous about preparation, I had, naturally, researched a lot about the Qur'an and its pronouncements on suffering, providence and what Islam had to say about the classic God and evil theodicy dilemma. But as this was meant to be a very personal film, rooted in my own quest and the discomfort precipitated by my lately deceased father, it was my cameraman's strong opinion that we were lacking spontaneity, emotion, surprise. I only discovered all this much later after I quizzed him about what precisely he had intended by putting me in that truck and getting me to ad lib to camera.

The logistics were really quite demanding. The terrain was so bumpy underneath the vehicle that we had to keep on filming and filming in the hope that stretches of twenty or thirty seconds were broadcastable. There was just myself and Bruno in the open space, and the driver who had a brief to keep driving around, not too quickly and with an eye for avoiding bumps in the road. We had been doing this for about half an hour. Rather typically I had been descriptive, offering a commentary on what we were seeing. Then Bruno changed gear with a question.

"How's all this affecting you?"

I caught the sight of a lone infant sitting in the remains of a house. He was trying to play with the remains of an old toy, but he was distracted. His heart wasn't really in it. He heard the sound of our car engine and looked up and stared me straight in the face. And that was all I needed to unlock the floodgates. For nearly nine days now, I had been holding back on the cumulative effect of what I was experiencing. Perhaps it was the impact of these last two days which had been almost exclusively focused on children and how they were, or were not, coping. Whatever it was it led to me recording the following words to camera.

"What's extraordinary is that when my dad looked at those TV pictures and said, 'what have those people done to deserve this?' I never thought I'd actually be sitting here looking at all this in such proximity, so close. It's really eerie as well, because there are so few people around. I mean, what's remarkable is the—the mixture of emotions it gives you. I mean, there's the kind of almost desperation you feel for the people who suffered and died. But you get these little nuances of—of optimism. You get the odd house sort of standing there and there's actually people living in these isolated structures."

I was aware of a lump in my throat and tears welling up. I tried to carry on and keep my composure. I was fighting a losing battle.

"There's a part of you, if you really wanted to let go, you'd just—you just start to cry. But maybe you don't do that on TV, because it's not the kind of thing that a macho reporter does. You know, you get these guys strolling around in their khakis looking all authoritative and they know what they're talking about and they're on top of the situation. But that's not how I feel now."

Many months later, when we came to assemble the footage and edit the whole program, I cringed as I saw myself breaking down on camera. It looked more worthy of an outburst by Gwyneth Paltrow at the Oscars than a television presenter. I suggested to Simon Ardizzone, our film editor, that we drop it.

"No," he said. "It's very powerful. Let's see what the Channel Four editor says when we show it to him on the first viewing." When Aaqil Ahmed came to see it some weeks later, he dabbed his eyes and had no doubts about its place in the film.

"If that was simply a news report, I'd have no doubts about saying 'take it out'. But it's a one-hundred-minute film. It's a personal story of exploration. Any human being with emotions on seeing what you had seen would react in a similar way. I'd say it is cathartic. You were crying for the whole audience." I think that was sound editorial judgment.

The TV presenter as lightning conductor. Looking back, I suspect that, at that time, I was also still grieving for my father and his mention in what I had to say had no small part to play in my emotions coming to the fore. But be that as it may, it represented a huge gear change in the feel of the film. And it wasn't to be the last time that this tsunami journey would reduce me to tears.

We had reached our final night in Aceh, and India was beckoning. We faced a tortuously complicated journey via Medan and Kuala Lumpur to get to Chennai in the southern state of Tamil Nadu for the next leg of our adventure. Our team gathered at the rickety Aceh Hotel and we had a farewell dinner of sorts. The indefatigable Fauzan had not put a foot wrong in all the time we had been here. Resourceful and good spirited, he had revealed a mine of local contacts built up over several months helping news networks from more than a dozen countries. He never once complained about the crazily long hours of our daily routine. A young man who could find you an Islamic geologist or a mechanical crane equipped with operator at the drop of a hat. As we parted in the hotel foyer, he took me to one side.

"I bought you something," he said. He reached inside a bag and produced a khaki-colored shirt with a small black logo on the upper left pocket. "It was only one dollar at the market, but I kind of figured you have a long journey ahead and you might already be running out of clothes." It was incredibly thoughtful. That shirt appeared many times on camera in India and later. To this day I still have it in my wardrobe and on the rare occasions when the temperature in the UK reaches twenty-five degrees centigrade or more, out it comes, flooding me with memories of Sumatra, of Fadil, and the faces of all those orphaned children.

After a hastily grabbed dinner on that last evening, Bruno called by my room. Our chat was briefly interrupted by the sound of the muezzin in the mosque opposite calling the faithful to night prayer. "It seems like we've been here ages," he said to me, placing his camera on a chair by the bed. "Is there anything else we should be filming before we pack up and leave first thing tomorrow? Any final thoughts or insights? A kind of wrap-up?" It was a good question.

"I don't know whether we will ever use it in the final cut of the film," I replied. "But I've come across this poem by a Tunisian author called Abu al-Qasim al-Shabbi."

"Great, let me fire up the camera," said Bruno hastily. We toned down the lighting in the room, closed the windows to filter out the noise of the passing traffic. I perched myself on the end of the bed and looked straight into the camera:

"Reflect, the order of life is a subtle, marvelous, unique order.

For nothing but death endears life and only the fear of tombs adorns it.

Were it not for the misery of painful life

People would not grasp the meaning of happiness.

Whomever the scowling of the dark does not terrify, does not feel the bliss of the new morning."[8]

8. Cited Ormsby, *Theodicy in Islamic*, 265.

These final words to camera in Aceh would turn out to be prophetic. A vision of existence in which humans enjoy the glories of sunsets but suffer at the hands of droughts and tornadoes, aspects of a material world that are ambiguous and interdependent, was a narrative still in its infancy. Much more along these lines was to emerge further down the road. That night, I slept fitfully, awoken again for the last time at 4.30 am by the call to prayer outside my bedroom window. By mid-morning, we had said our farewells and were on our way to southern India, to Tamil Nadu, for my first ever visit to that great country.

3

India

Measuring the Ocean with a Spoon

OUR JOURNEY TO INDIA was almost torpedoed before we even boarded the plane for Chennai. We had departed London nearly two weeks before without visas to enter the country. The office had sent off our applications to the Indian High Commission in London in what we thought was good time, but just a few days before we were due to leave, the phone call to have the visas issued still hadn't come through. Our entry visa for Indonesia had been acquired in good time and was securely in our passports. We were told that we didn't require one for Thailand, but what would happen if India House just kept on delaying? We would miss our departure date and endanger the whole shoot. In the week before departure our production manager, Jessica Ross, took the team to one side.

"Look, this is crazy," she said. "We're just waiting for a call and I can bike the passports over and get them stamped but we can't leave it until the day before you leave and risk it. There's only one thing for it, you've all got to get a second passport." Her thinking was that we would travel on our current passports and then, when the call came through from the Indian High Commission, long after we had departed London, she would use the second passports for the visas and then get them to us in Aceh before we flew for India. It seemed like a good plan. Passport offices will issue a second copy to journalists in exceptional circumstances. For years I had had two passports: one with an Israeli stamp in it and another for travelling around the Middle East to countries like Syria, Libya, and Saudi Arabia

44

where the Jewish state is not recognized and where the sight of an Israeli entry visa is an effective bar of entry to that country. Unfortunately, one of my passports had lapsed and so another was required. The rest of the crew also needed a backup.

It seemed a good plan in theory. But confidence in the wonders of DHL and Federal Express can be overstated, especially when courier companies need to deliver to totally remote places like Banda Aceh. With only four days before our proposed departure date from Indonesia, we still didn't have our visas for India. Jess spoke to me from the London office.

"Look, I really have a bad feeling about this," she told me. "Fedex are saying they can't guarantee delivery by the date we need and it's the same for all the other couriers." She had a plan B. This one really was a rabbit out of the hat. "There's no other option. I am coming to meet you when you change planes in Kuala Lumpur and I'll bring the visas with me."

A return flight to Malaysia just to drop off passports? It sounded a tad excessive, but the alternative was to cancel the proposed filming for all of the next three weeks and to set it up again at a later date. Logistically speaking, that did not bear thinking about. So, Jess's plan was put into action. Her flight was due into Kuala Lumpur late afternoon and our flight to Chennai on the eastern coast of India was not until two or three hours later. Of course, any big delays and we would have been scuppered. However, our flight from Medan landed on time and when we touched down, we got an SMS message from Jess informing us that she had arrived safely and was hovering around inside the airport terminal. All was going to plan. Or so we thought.

Our team was effectively in transit. All our cases and equipment had been checked in on leaving Banda Aceh two flights earlier and had been transferred automatically to the Air India flight, and so we remained "airside" throughout. Jess, on the other hand, had entered Malaysian territory by clearing customs and immigration with her bags and was now inside the airport proper. We couldn't exit our position as we wouldn't have been able to get back inside to board our flight. But neither could she reach us without a boarding pass. She was planning to spend the weekend in the Malaysian capital before returning to London, so she was forty-eight hours away from acquiring her boarding pass. We exchanged frantic messages by SMS and then she called.

"This is crazy. I've been explaining to the airport people here that I need to get you your passports. They just shrug their shoulders and shoo me away. It's maddening. What about you guys, can you get past security?" After talking further, we directed Jess around to the part of the airport terminal where we were based. Then, out of nothing, she appeared miraculously on the other side of a secured glass screen. So near but so far. She examined inside her belongings and produced the passports, waving them around in front of us on the other side of the glass. "Wait there," we mouthed exaggeratedly through the glass. We wandered over to some officials who were guarding an exit door and pulled one of them over towards the glass panel. Jess continued to wave the passports around madly as if she was waving the checkered flag at the end of the Indianapolis 500.

"We need to meet our friend to get our visas for India," I hollered.

"But you already have passports," he said, pointing to the burgundy-colored documents in our hands. Not good. It must have looked as though we were embarking on a dose of international passport fraud. I produced a business card with my name and "journalist" on it, a word which, thankfully, he recognized. He looked at us. Then over to Jess's plaintive face on the other side of the screen. "OK," he said. "Come this way." We went over to his station near the exit sign. After he asked for our passports, he filled out three slips of paper with our names and ID numbers on them. "Show these later when you pass back through," he said. Taking his time, he reached out for a small stamper and left an imprint on the three slips of paper. "Go," he said with an unambiguous wave of his hand away from his body.

We arrived on the eastern coast of India late at night, after a two-and-a-half-hour flight, and were greeted in Chennai by our next location producer. Fauzan in Aceh had now been replaced by Neelima. Everything about her manner in those first few minutes exuded confidence and competence. She was a woman in her late forties perhaps, decidedly diminutive at barely five feet tall, with very large brown eyes and shoulder-length dark hair. She strode ahead of us, clasping documents, waving them at officials and generally wearing down any apparatchik who threatened to make our stay in the airport one second longer than was strictly necessary. On leaving the airport building, we were effortlessly shoveled into a large van. "Now we go to hotel. Tomorrow will take care of itself with visit to temple," she said. "You all need to sleep." How right she was. It was like having Mum in charge of the shoot. After the rickety, crumbling uncertainties of the Aceh Hotel, now here we were in a very smart four-star hotel in Chennai. When I entered my room after finally winning my personal battle with the electronically operated key card, I opened the door and thought I had died and gone to heaven. Bowls of fruit on the tables. A dressing-gown! Was that a *chocolate* on my pillow? What exotic pleasures were these? No matter. Within minutes I was on the bed and out cold. I awoke, hours later, with brown creamy liquid in my ear.

India had suffered more than ten and a half thousand casualties on its eastern coast in the tsunami and a further five thousand people were unaccounted for in the nearby Andaman and Nicobar Islands. I would soon be visiting refugee camps and encountering parents who had had their children ripped from their grasp by the killer wave. But before these meetings, I wanted to get some context. India was not Indonesia. Everywhere we looked from our vehicle on our first full day, we saw temples galore with faces and depictions of deities. Their faces were all blue. "That is because blue is the symbol of the immeasurable and the infinite," said Neelima, craning her neck around from the front seat to address us. It was a far cry from Aceh's Islamic austerity with its emphasis on no images or depictions of the divine.

We had an early start, on our way to an appointment with a Professor Bhaskaran from Tamil Nadu University. I had signaled in advance to Neelima that one area I wanted to explore on my visit was whether it was at all sensible to ask the question as to whether Hinduism could be classified as a polytheistic or monotheistic faith. At a very basic level, it appeared to be the former. A cursory digest of textbooks in preparation for the film shoot had introduced me to major figures such as Vishnu, Lord Krishna, Shiva, Parvati, Kali and Ganesha. Web-based searches had thrown up arresting headlines such as "the thirty-three million gods of Hinduism".[1] Much of the confusion appears to stem from the ambiguity in translating the Sanskrit term "*trayastrimsatikoti*", which is found in a number of Vedic texts. The word "koti" lends itself to either "type" or "supreme". You can see where the problem occurs. If "type" is taken to mean separate unit or entity, then we have an explosion of deities. I have even seen reference to there being three hundred and thirty million gods! All this was of great significance to me. The classic problem articulated by my father on Boxing Day evening was predicated on there being just one God, loving in nature and well-disposed to humanity. But if there were hundreds of thousands of gods, none of whom had supreme responsibility for the creation of the world, then the classic theodicy dilemma didn't really arise. Which is not

---

1. *Huffington Post*, October 12, 2012.

to say that Hindus would not have any opinions on suffering, how it comes into the world, and how to make sense of it.

We had a long drive of several hours down to Thanjavur to the Brihadisvara Temple, a magnificent conical structure built under the reign of Tamil King, Raja Raja Chola, between 1003 and 1010 CE. When it revealed its golden bronze brickwork to us, immediately my mind turned to images of the ancient Ziggurats of Mesopotamia I had seen in drawings on numerous history films. This yellowy-brown masterpiece looked extraordinary, set back against the deep blue sky. It rose from the ground and the closer we got to it, the greater the detail came into focus: hundreds and hundreds of images, gargoyles, faces, and figures all encrusted in the exterior rising up from above the main temple door.

Before Professor Bhaskaran arrived, Bruno wanted to execute a few establishing shots of me arriving at the temple. He was now relieved of his camera and full-time director role as Neelima had informed us that we had a local cameraman alongside us for this leg of the journey. I'm not sure if Bruno appreciated the break from the arduous work of shooting on camera himself or regretted the loss, but he and Nandha both had the idea of filming me strolling across the expansive tiled precinct which led towards the main entrance. It was a fine idea, in principle. The problem was the temperature outside was nearing forty degrees centigrade. The baking sun was beating down on the pavement ahead of us. You could have fried an egg on it. Then came the words I did not want to hear. "You'll have to take your shoes and socks off as it's a holy site," said Neelima. Everybody else was observing these rules of approach, despite the scorching temperatures. I looked at the people shuffling across the huge, tiled area, then prepared myself. None of them was flinching or showing any sign of discomfort.

I removed my shoes and socks and took my instructions. I was to emerge from a shaded area, into the line of the camera and then weave my way down, about fifty meters in all, through a line of pilgrims, and disappear into the black hole which was the main entrance. Technically it was a devil of a shot to execute for the camera. First there was the change from shade to full exposure. Then there were the depth of field adjustments as the focus would have to be constantly revised to keep me clearly defined in shot as I moved ever further away. Straying members of the public would be another hindrance as they would walk into shot and obscure the cameraman's line of vision. In all, the take took *six attempts*. Have you any idea what the soles of my feet felt like by the end of the last effort? Religious fanatics braving hot coals have suffered less. A voice from my mother came constantly into my head: "Offer it up for the Holy Souls in Purgatory."

We had gone way past lunchtime and my nerves were jangling. The tightening vise around my temple was a hunger headache. A constant supply of bananas and bottled water had kept this at bay since 6 am, but now I did something totally out of character. I threw a prima donna tantrum and refused to do anything more until we sat down and ate. This is when I discovered the wonders of working with a local crew. Sabbu, our delightfully tubby and upbeat Tamil sound recordist, took me by the arm and led me past a long line of queuing Thanjavur citizens. We were queue-jumping at the local restaurant. "BBC," he shouted as onlookers gazed at us passing along the line. (Not strictly true, as we were "Channel Four UK", not the BBC. But no-one seemed to mind.) Once inside, hands were washed thoroughly at a sink in the corner, huge green leaves from banana trees were laid out as plates on our table. We ate vegetables and rice with our hands.

"Don't drink the water from the jug," screamed Neelima, just as I forgetfully raised a glass to my lips. "Here. Rinse that with bottled water. We can't risk a presenter with 'Delhi Belly' on day one." We ate like this for the next week or so. The food was delicious without exception. The locals gawped at Bruno and me as though we had landed from another planet.

"Is that Mr. Bean?" I heard one of the staff ask, pointing at me. This followed me around for the rest of the week. It wasn't the first, nor the last time I had been likened to the silent comic character portrayed on our TV and cinema screens by the actor, Rowan Atkinson.

I desperately craved a post-prandial nap, but the Brihadisvara temple beckoned once more. Now at least the crew had a sense of what it was like to prance across those scorched paving slabs in bare feet, even if they didn't have to do five retakes. Once inside, we came across a very patient Professor Bhaskaran, dressed in a smart matching light-brown two-piece tunic top and trousers. He had been waiting for almost two hours by all accounts. Our guru was eager to take us on a tour to the many shrines dotted around the temple interior. As we strolled around, I asked him about the main query I had about Hinduism's status as a polytheistic or monotheistic religion. Even on this very first full day we had seen images of different gods in shops, on street corners, pasted inside cars on window screens and even inside the myriad of tiny yellow and green tuk tuks, the tiny autorickshaws that darted around between bigger vehicles on the saturated roads. Frequently, as the filthy exhaust fumes dissipated away, a god's face would come slowly into view. Always blue.

"It does look polytheistic at first, but I would say that Hindus have a strong sense of the monotheistic too," he said, pointing up to the ceiling and some artwork that represented the whole cosmos. "Apart from the many family gods and other related gods, they also have a strong sense of ultimate Supreme Being or Power." When I pressed him further, he talked about a creator god, Brahma, which predated many of the "big guns" like Vishnu and Shiva and, closely related to this, the notion of *brahman* which the Professor talked of as "ultimate reality". It rang a bell. I later went back to my notes and found an entry that spoke of it as a "single binding unity behind diversity in all that exists in the universe". Spokes on a bicycle wheel all coming back to the central hub if you will. Then I recalled, from my discussions in Aceh, those ninety-nine names for Allah in the Qur'an: dimensions, aspects of an ultimate Godhead. It seemed that although Hinduism was far from being a classic "Abrahamic" faith, it could neither be crudely categorized as pure polytheism.

The eager professor was clearly rising to his challenge. I surmised from his incredibly smart and rather formal clothes that this was an encounter he had really been quite looking forward to. It was deeply touching to see someone so eager to assist us and make sure we didn't fall prey to any misunderstandings. The key Vedic concepts were now flying thick and fast.

"*Atman* is central to Hindu thought," he said as we passed by a small elephant that was accepting bank notes as offerings in its curled-up trunk and then returning the gesture with a neat tap on the donor's forehead. "In our view of the world, all living things, plants, trees, animals, and humans are connected in a web of life, of spirit, by *atman*. It is indestructible, so when a creature dies, this *atman* or spirit is reabsorbed after reincarnation. And so the cycle of life and death goes on."

I wanted to know about karma. What did this have to do with reincarnation? Were people caught up in the tsunami somehow caught up in this karmic dynamic? The word literally means, "action" and although there are variations within Hindu philosophy as well as in the schools of Buddhism and Jainism, there is a fundamental lying at the heart of it: causality. Good actions and thoughts herald good outcomes and the same with the negatives. So, working backwards, a bad outcome (such as drowning in a tsunami) is, in a sense, the logical outcome of previous bad actions. You reap what you sow. Except that many young children I knew had died in the

Boxing Day tsunami, so how, I wanted to know from the learned professor, did that work? What could a four-year-old possibly have done "karmically" to merit such an outcome?

"Such children could well have done wrong in a previous life," said the Professor. "This is what some people are saying with regard to young children who are deaf and dumb, that they suffer in this life for what went before." To the politically correct western mind, this stuff is utterly un-orthodox and unacceptable. I reminded the learned scholar of the story of Glenn Hoddle, a hugely successful English soccer player and manager, who had fallen under the influence of faith healer Eileen Drewery in the 1990s. In an interview with a national newspaper entitled "Hoddle Puts His Faith in God and England", he had conceded he had a belief that "the disabled, and others, are being punished for sins in a former life."[2] In February 1999 the subsequent outcry from disability groups and politicians cost Hoddle his job as coach to the England soccer team. The key fracture in eastern and western thought is reincarnation. Because Hindus believe that spirit is reborn after death, it makes total sense to hold to the view that the spiritual life of an infant inherits the previous karmic account of the adult person who had died. God help the child who is unlucky enough to scoop the soul of a Hitler, Stalin or Pol Pot in the karma lottery. I concede to being disturbed by these thoughts, but there was still a lot more I wanted to ask of Professor Bhaskaran.

We wandered into the very large shrine dedicated to the god Shiva. I had seen the central image of a deity with many cartwheeling hands and limbs, engaged in a vigorous dance which, I learned, was called a *tandava*.

"This represents the many qualities of Shiva," the professor told me, pointing ahead to a man who was lighting a candle and placing it in front of the image as an offering. The pilgrim lit several joss sticks, placed the candle in a small metal bowl and made gyratory movements with it before placing it in front of the figure and bowing in prayer. "His qualities are creation, preservation, destruction, obscuration, and grace." The scholar told me he took "obscuration" to mean hiddenness, and this made sense as someone who knew the Psalms well: "Why do you hide your face and forget our affliction and oppression?" asks the psalmist.[3]

"So, these qualities are all held in unity within the one deity, not sepa-rated?" I asked.

2. *The Times* January 30, 1999.

3. Ps 44:24.

"That is so," came the reply. "He is doing all of these actions. He must do this, to make the world move." I wasn't to know it at the time, but rather like that frustrating conversation in Aceh with the geologist who declined to be drawn on the whole question of why tectonic plates were essential in Allah's plan for the world, Shiva's unifying of the forces of creation and destruction would be a theme I would come back to revisit many months down the road of this intriguing exploration.

The following day we put Thanjavur and that quite extraordinary temple behind us and headed back to the coast to a town by the beguiling name of Naggapattinam. It had been settled by Portuguese sea traders, and fishing is to this day the main motor of the local economy. The lion's share of India's tsunami victims emanated from here. Many of the local casualties had been fishermen and their families. Neelima had organized a visit to a local refugee camp.

"This is going to be an interesting day for you," she promised. "Two women, with very different views about life after the tsunami," she said with a glint in her eye.

"Do they know one another? Are they friends?" I asked.

"No. I don't think so. First we need to find Ramayee."

The Agarapeti camp had been sponsored by an outfit called the Art of Living Foundation. Established in 1981 by spiritual guru, Sri Sri Ravi Shankar, this philanthropic charity now has representation in dozens of countries internationally. On arrival, my mind flashed back to the makeshift shanty towns we had seen in Sumatra. Flimsy sheets of corrugated iron had been hastily thrown up everywhere. Washing lines crisscrossed everywhere the eye could see. Scantily clad children played in puddles of dirty water. A brown and white mongrel dog shuffled around awkwardly. One of its rear legs had been broken, presumably in a collision with a vehicle, and it dragged its broken limb behind it like some burdensome relative.

"This way," shouted Neelima, getting directions from one of the refugee camp assistants who was helping us locate Ramayee. We turned a corner and there she was. A young woman in her late twenties I would have guessed, wearing a respectable but very worn yellowy-brown sari. She clasped her hands together and smiled at us and then bowed. After introductions she bade us all enter her makeshift shelter. The first thing I spotted as she crossed the threshold was a photo of a young boy, placed next to a small image of a temple god with a light flickering next to it. I asked Ramayee to tell me what had happened to him.

"My boss's son was shouting, 'water is coming.' I came out and I saw it coming with great speed. It was the height of three palm trees." She used her hands to point upwards to the skies. "I was then taken by the force of the water. It hurled me towards a temple and there, I managed to thrust out my arm and grab a metal gate with my hand." Ramayee now hung on tightly for dear life as scores of other bodies washed past her.

But what had become of her child? "When the water eventually subsided," she told me, "a small girl from our neighborhood was sitting upstairs. She was holding onto my little daughter. She said to me: 'Your child is lost.'" This was Dinesh, the serious-looking boy in the picture frame. He had the biggest, brownest eyes you can ever imagine. The face of an angel. I could not take my eyes off him for quite some time, partly because he had such an alluring face and complexion, but also partly out of fear. Why fear? Because I was so overcome with sadness that I dreaded having to suddenly engage Ramayee and talk to her about her darling Dinesh.

I finally took a deep breath and turned around. I was totally unprepared for what I saw. Ramayee was beaming away from ear to ear with the look of someone who had just accepted a proposal of marriage. She caressed her remaining child, her seven-year-old daughter, and started to chat to me, via our translator and sound recordist, Subbu. "Many people have died in the world, and my boy is just one of them," she told me calmly, still with that radiant smile on her face. "So, I am not angry with God. God has given and God has taken away. I see many children around who look like Dinesh. So, I think I am being shown them for a purpose. I see him in them." I noted how effortlessly she was comfortable using the word "God". It was not "the gods" or "the deities", or "spirits". Pervading so many of her answers was a strong sense of the spiritual being found everywhere in everything. With great sincerity and conviction, she had a simple formula for conveying to me what had happened to her son in the tsunami. "God has gone to God," she said. The smile became even more pervasive. I can still picture her face to this day.

The Art of Living Foundation provided sessions of meditation to assist the refugees in overcoming their traumas, and we took our technical equipment along to film one such event. Ramayee participated and was totally oblivious to the presence of the camera as she squatted on the stone floor and joined around two dozen or so other refugees under the supervision of an experienced charity official. Eyes closed, hands facing outwards, she joined the chorus of those chanting *Om*, the cosmic sound of the universe.[4]

Ramayee was still beaming away when we said our farewells to her and her daughter. "Wasn't she amazing?" I quipped to Neelima. "Not a hint of self-pity, or that inevitable question, 'Why me?'"

"Many Indians are quite fatalistic," she said. "What will happen will happen. Everything has a reason. But I think you are going to find the next interview quite different."

That was something of an understatement. In the very same refugee camp, just three or four blocks away, lived a woman in her early thirties. Her name was Poonguzhali. When we meandered through children playing in the mud, and various livestock, we finally located her shelter. What a contrast with Ramayee. No smile, merely a very worn, severe face. I raised my hand in a greeting and she nodded, modestly, back. Inside her dwelling she told me the brutal facts. On the day in question, at around 9 am, she had been collecting water close to her house.

"Neighbors began screaming: 'water is coming, water is coming. You must run.'" Her husband and three of her children were away, tending to their small shop nearby in the town. "The water crashed in suddenly," she told me, "and I was swept onto the roof of a nearby house. I fell unconscious." Poonguzhali has no idea for how long she was out cold, but when she came to, she was met with the most horrific sight. "They had laid my husband out next to me. He was barely alive, so we rushed him to the hospital. I remember he was foaming at the mouth." She pointed to her own mouth and then picked up her story. "He battled as best he could, but it was too late. He died on the way to hospital. Then, around midday, I learned the news that two of my children had also been taken by the wave." At this point, she turned to a young girl next to her, her only remaining child, Vimila. "She survived only because she was not here." For some time, we all just sat there in silence. "At that time, I honestly felt like taking my own life and joining my husband and my children," she told me.

I did my best to convey our condolences without resorting to those ghastly clichés oft borne by hurried journalists. Then I asked her about how all this had impacted on her faith. "We used to do everything, believing in God," she said. "But as all of them have died, my faith in God has gone."

---

4. This sound is first mentioned in the Upanishads, the mystical texts associated with the Vedanta philosophy, written between 800 and 600 BCE.

This was the first person on this journey who had expressed such stark sentiments. But had she ceased to believe in God completely?

"God is there, but I have lost my trust in him," she said defiantly. "Because he couldn't save my husband and my children." Then she uttered three words I had never before heard in my life. "I hate God."

There's no rejoinder, no easy formula to fall back on when someone says such words to you. Especially when they are sitting opposite you framed by photo images of their recently deceased husband and children. There was a pregnant silence during which Poonghuzali turned to her remaining child, Vimila, and pulled her closer towards her in a gesture of mutual comfort. We ended our time with this poor woman by filming a short sequence of her at work in a nearby garment factory. She was processing fabric on a machine in a scene that reminded me of some old 1950s photos my mother used to show me of my aunts in the textile mills in Lancashire in the north of England. I watched her attentively. It was clear she was a skilled and expert manipulator of cloth. She appeared totally unaware of the presence of the camera as she got down to her task of measuring, cutting and then carefully stitching.

God is there, but I have lost my trust in him, she had said to me. Her devastating misfortune had not led her to tell me that God did not exist, or that her wretched experience rendered belief in such a power impossible. No, Poonghuzali had made offerings to a variety of Hindu gods in the past in the hope that she and her family would be protected. Her anger was they had utterly defaulted on their side of the contract. Where had they been? How could they have allowed three people so close to her to go to such an awful death after years and years of supplication and loyalty? This dynamic has an equivalent strand in the Judeo-Christian tradition. One thinks of the anger in the Psalms:

"Awake, Lord! Why do you sleep? Rouse yourself!

Do not reject us forever. Why do you hide your face and forget our misery and oppression?"[5]

Other psalms voice resentment at how the wicked flourish and how the just man appears to suffer, abandoned by God:

"My God, my God, why have you forsaken me?

Why are you so far from saving me, so far from the words of my groaning?

5. Ps 44:23–24.

O my God, I cry out by day, but you do not answer."[6]

Parallels between relationships between human beings and with God can be inexact at the best of times, but it can be argued that anger is, in a way, an expression of investment, engagement. If your partner cares enough to voice his or her ire with you, although it may indeed be early signs of potential difficulties, it is surely better than total disengaged apathy. In such circumstances what was once a strong, intimate connection is in a state of unhealthy atrophy and on its way to wasting away, of withering on the vine. When we departed the refugee camp, I was still consumed with pity for this unfortunate woman and her daughter, but not a little envious of her anger. It suggested an aliveness and a sense of passion that has often eluded me in my own spiritual quest. It is possibly dangerous to put too much emphasis on subjective feeling, but so much of the time, prayer has felt very one-sided. I can't be the only person who has been racked with doubts about there "being anybody *there*", a lot of the time.

Looking back at the time in India, some of the most memorable conversations and encounters actually occurred as we traveled to and from locations. Countless exchanges took place between our London-based team and Neelima, Subbu on sound, and Nandha who was filming for us. They were intrigued by my fascination, nay near *obsession*, with karma. In particular the relationship between karma and reincarnation.

"Spirit or atman is imperishable," insisted Subbu, as we slalomed around a handful of unpredictable tuk tuks in our people carrier. "The spirit must go somewhere after death."

"But," I retorted eagerly, "if the spirit is joined with God, or 'supreme spirit', then there is your answer. Like Ramayee said of her son, 'God has gone to God.'" Subbu was less than impressed.

"No, no. That is only when you achieve *moksha*." Goodness me, another term for me to get to grips with.

"What on earth is *moksha*?" I asked him. Subbu explained that this is a transcendental state, a release, or freedom, from being reborn and is only possible after an individual has achieved such positive karma that they escape the constant cycle of reincarnation. If you were not good enough to secure this state, following physical death, your spirit has to be reborn into another being. And how or where you reappear in the next life following death, is very much determined by one's karma in the current life. I wanted to somehow convey all this in our film, but that was quite a production

6. Ps 22:1–2.

challenge. Making religious documentaries can be difficult enough at the best of times with so much emphasis on the abstract. I had lost count of the number of times in my editing suite that I had resorted to falling back on pictures of clouds and sunsets when I was talking about God. Maybe Muslims had got this right after all with their insistence that Godhead should bear no physical representation. One certainly struggled with television, which relies so extensively on imagery. Radio and print of course are much less of a challenge and are easier bedfellows in matters theological, as they lend themselves more easily to the abstract. Then I stumbled across an idea. "Can we find a really big hotel with two or three elevators?" I asked the production team. "A real skyscraper number, with all those floor numbers illuminated on panels next to the sliding doors."

Sure enough, we found such a place. What I had in mind was using the various ascending and descending floors to represent one's karmic progressions . . . moving either up or down in the life chain. Although not common, it is thought by some Hindus that humans who commit really bad actions can be reincarnated "lower" down the order and take on animal form. While this might be construed as "punishment", those who subscribe to this view insist it is simply an account of the way things are, like a set of scientific or mechanical laws. I set about explaining all this from inside a hotel elevator, much to the consternation of fellow passengers who were sharing the space with our small team. This being India, when I had raised the notion of "permissions" to film with Neelima, she gave her characteristic head roll which I had taken to mean, "yes of course, I get the idea". But then, a sudden change of tack. "Oh no," she said. "This would take weeks and weeks. Committees, meetings, phone calls inside the hotel chain management. We just go in, do the filming, and leave as smartly as possible. If anyone asks any questions, I will be in the lobby to deal with it."

I can't imagine what impression we made on clients who were waiting for the doors to open, only to be greeted with a rather fired-up Englishman likening the theory of karma and reincarnation to moving up and down the floors of the hotel in an elevator. Because we had to do several retakes, we weren't as speedy as we would have wished and had to bluff our way out of the hotel foyer by charming the hotel management and smiling a lot in their direction. But the sequence was now "in the can". Every time I see this section of our film played back, it brings a smile to my face.

Discussions with our Indian crew members about the pros and cons of karma continued. And we were now setting off on a trip to pursue this theme of enquiry further with one of the country's most celebrated gurus. The Art of Living Foundation had its base in Bangalore. Thrillingly, this involved a ten-and-a-half-hour overnight train ride from Tamil Nadu before we could meet up with its founder, Sri Sri Ravi Shankar. India boasts the third largest railway system in the world, accounting for more than eight and a half billion passenger journeys annually. Its rolling stock is enormous: seventy-four thousand train passenger wagons and more than twelve thousand locomotives. One of them, the Myesore Express, was waiting for us in Thanjavur at 6 pm. The scene on the platform was like some excerpt from E.M. Forster's *Passage to India*. Scores of makeshift railway porters almost outnumbered the passengers. Neelima had lined up an army of helpers outside the station concourse, and I could see and hear her haggling with them. Lots of shaking of the head. Voices were raised. She affected to walk away and break off negotiations; a woman who obviously drove a hard bargain. But once a fee was agreed, out came her magic bag with a stash of rupee notes and we were off, a veritable caravansary marching intently through the station and out towards the platform for departure. A sea of imploring faces now greeted us as food and bottled drinks were thrust in front of us. I gave into temptation, broke all the ground rules about buying "street food", and started to scoff down two samosas. I earned a gentle rebuke from our local producer.

"You want to spend all night on loo?" she asked, with a wink in her eye.

"It's only vegetable," I replied. It had been unwise of me to give into my ravenous appetite, but thankfully there were no dire consequences in the "Montezuma's Revenge/Delhi Belly" department.

Neelima had been impeccably well organized and had secured us all sleeper berths in an air-conditioned carriage. The fare equivalent was less than ten dollars per head. But the really unforgettable aspect of this journey was the ticketing. Our local producer had all our passes in her hand, shaped like a fan. They had to be presented to an official waiting alongside the train.

"Can't they just check them once we are on the train?" I asked her. This was greeted with a look of incredulity.

"You clearly have never taken a train in India before," she exclaimed. "Trains are famous for people climbing on without ticket. How would you feel if someone was sleeping in your bed?" This turned out to be quite a prophetic question.

The next stage of the boarding process revealed precisely why the tickets were essential. We approached our train carriage at the rear of the platform and there to the left of the door was a piece of card inserted into a small postbox-shaped panel. It was a white document with what appeared to be a list inscribed on it. On closer inspection, I could see each of our individual names! There were a dozen passengers in all, and the train official had to cross-check our tickets with the names on the panel before we boarded. Such amazing organization. I am not sure precisely why it was so thrilling, but to see "Mr. Mark Dowd: Carriage 11: Cabin 2:3L" emblazoned on the side of an impressive Indian locomotive was really quite something. "3L" was the highest of three beds/left side, as each cabin was divided into six beds each, three on either side.

The Myesore Express trundled off on time. For the next two hours I glimpsed the lengthening shadows on the flat, unfolding plains of Tamil Nadu. Occasional beasts of burden came into view with their owners on nearby dusty roads which caught the last glints of the setting sun. They carried anything from sacks of vegetables to materials precariously balanced on wooden pallets. Back on board, Neelima had shopped for an impromptu dinner which we consumed in her compartment, and by 10 pm it was time to brush teeth, ram in the wax earplugs and hope that ours was a snoring-free zone.

It took me an hour or so to nod off as I was initially too excited to sleep. There is something about hearing the sound of the train chassis and the occasional grinding of wheels on track that brings out the inner child in you. I pondered the idea of the gentle rocking motion being a throwback to fetal memories of the womb. Then, in the darkness, a face was suddenly conjured up out of nowhere. Poonghuzali was back with me again. A stern, serious expression that posed questions. How would I have reacted if that had been me? It's fanciful and not a little romantic to bleat out assurances about how such experiences might "mold" us and forge strength of character. But, faced with the crippling sense of loss, would my own faith have survived? It didn't take long to move onto an even more searching probe. Fast forward the videotape of my life to those final moments, just like I had posed the question in my encounter with Richard Dawkins. Staring down the barrel of consciousness being extinguished, if his "wobble" had been that God may yet be a reality, post-death, that he might reluctantly have to grapple with, my equivalent discomforting realization might be that all that lay before me was nothingness. Ceasing. To. Exist. Not rebirth, or a harmonious joining with a spiritual entity or plane immensely deeper than oneself. Simple nihilistic obliteration. It hasn't happened very often in my life, but in the few episodes when such thoughts have erupted, the mind goes into a swirl of near panic, breathing becomes short and snatched and then slowly, one reverts. I thought back to those meditation scenes we had filmed in the refugee camp and made a deliberate effort to take long, deep intakes of breath.

It must have worked. I was then out like a light. Until that is, a twinging sensation in the nether regions awoke me around 2 am. What a time to be caught short. I couldn't even remember where the restroom was. I recalled that it was at the end of our carriage, but in which direction? I gently clambered down the short ladder from my top bunk. I was still half-asleep, and my powers of cognition were barely half-engaged. I found a small toilet, duly relieved myself, but on turning around and looking down the long corridor of the carriage, I suffered a total memory lapse. I knew I had emerged from a cabin in the center, but had my dormitory compartment been situated on the right or on the left? I had a fifty-fifty chance of either reclaiming my bunk, or giving someone the shock of their life. I took one last hard stare and convinced myself, no, it wasn't to the right, it was the left-hand side. I slid back the cabin door gently and plunged myself back into the darkness, groping for the ladder next to the bed. Up I went and was just about to hurl myself horizontally back onto my bed when I was gripped, quite literally, by a strange sensation. A hand clasped around my right ankle, pulling firmly. At this point, a figure on the top bunk sprung to life and switched on a torch. The hand was still around my leg. Three seconds later, the passenger in the bunk was shining a light in my face.

"What are you doing?" said a middle-aged man with a shock of dark hair and big brown eyes. I looked behind me, and there was Nandha, our cameraman.

"Mr. Bean, what are you doing?" he asked. "You're with us on the other side!" The man in the bunk heard this, stared at me, and smiled.

"Mr. Bean," he said. "I like it." A more than passing likeness to one of the world's most celebrated comics had made this an early, sure-fire nickname with the local crew that had stuck from day one. Coming up with this now gave us a bit of light relief in what would have been an otherwise tense situation. My sleep victim simply pulled over his blanket, made an outward "shooing" gesture with his hand, and I retired gracefully, with my tail between my legs. Five seconds more of that and there may have been quite a commotion.

Somewhat bleary-eyed, we pulled into Bangalore at 6.30 am, ran the gauntlet of more railway station sherpas, and made our way to the ashram at the Art of Living Foundation for our meeting with one of India's most renowned gurus. I had made a cursory examination of Gurudev Sri Sri Ravi Shankar's website for his world-famous meditation and yoga center, and come across the following words of his:

> A wise one is happy even in bad times. And the foolish one is unhappy even in good times. Spirituality is nothing out of the world. There is no division between what is spiritual, and what is material. Attaining a spiritual level is simply recognizing that there is life everywhere, that there is spirit everywhere.[7]

I was determined to have one last go at the karma question. After freshening up, we ascended the hundreds of steps towards our guru's main residence. From the throngs of crowds gathered excitedly outside, you'd think we'd come to talk to Michael Jackson or Beyoncé. Hundreds of devotees were kept at bay by a posse of no-nonsense security officials. Neelima used all the force her diminutive frame would muster to forge a "Red Sea" channel through them all, playing the "BBC" card at the top of her voice once more to great effect. The crowds parted and we climbed the steep steps to a distinctive ornate building ahead. There, wrapped in a white shroud, was a man whose face I had seen bearing down on me from a dozen or more posters in refugee camps and streets during the past week. Sri Sri Ravi Shankar had long flowing black hair and a carefully trimmed beard. A small man, I immediately sensed an individual who was comfortable in his own body. As he greeted us and swept us into his living room, I noticed a light, almost feminine voice which was at once gentle and reassuring. On the far side of the room was a panoply of more than a hundred or so objects which had all been carefully arranged on a table for a kaleidoscopic display.

"Most of these are gifts given to me from my many visits and speaking engagements," he said. I pointed to two very prominent mini-statues, side by side. "If you see Buddha and Ganesha together, they both have large stomachs," he remarked, pointing to the sizeable paunches on both the figures. "That is a sign of joy," he added, with a huge smile on his face. "You have to have a big tummy to demonstrate you are really happy. Like Santa Claus you know."

7. https://www.srisriravishankar.org/work/spirituality-human-values/art-of-living-foundation.

He bade me sit down on the floor and, with both of us now cross-legged, we began the karma interrogation. I pointed out how unfair it was for a child to effectively start a new life with a "negative bank account" by inheriting the negatives of a previous person's life.

"This is true, but it is not all fate and destiny," he insisted. "That child also has free will and every infant has a spark of divine light in them." But as many additional questions poured forth, I detected a smiling, perhaps mildly pitying expression coming my way across the carpet as this inquisitive westerner posed question after question.

"Look, there is a saying in the Upanishads, 'you cannot measure the ocean with a spoon." At this point he thrust out his hand and imitated the measuring action of a tiny spoon in his hand. "But you can throw the spoon into the ocean. In the same way, with a little intellect, you cannot understand everything in the universe, but what you can do is live the mysteries of life to the full."

It may have been my sensitivity, but when he said "with a *little* intellect", was he meaning with a modicum of analytical brainpower or was he implying, "with a limited mind like yours"? Ours was a wide-ranging and discursive exchange covering many areas, but it was when we got to the question of suffering and its place in the world that our man really had my hackles rising.

"There is a part for suffering on our planet," he contended. "Suppose we have no problems, then all the good qualities will disappear. The tsunami had one good thing you know. Human values got a boost." I had heard this argument many times and the more I heard it, the more it vexed me. I am sure Poonghuzali wasn't exactly popping the champagne corks at the thought that the destructive wave which swept her husband and children away had allowed international relief workers in to demonstrate their philanthropic virtues around her refugee camp. I think my mentor sensed my irritation. I couldn't let this pass unchallenged.

"I don't like the idea that young children in Thailand, Indonesia, and India have to suffer just so Europeans and Americans can jet in and show how compassionate they are," I said. I knew I had raised my voice and was almost shouting. It was utterly in contrast to my host's gracious, understated demeanor. I cited the case of the poor woman we had interviewed and her understandable reaction of anger.

"I know, I know," said the man opposite, running fingers studiedly through his beard. "There are a few people who might feel like that, but in the course of time, they come back."

I wasn't so sure.

Later that day we accompanied our leader to a huge mushroom shaped hall at the top of a hill. This was the central meeting place at the ashram. The word itself comes from the Sanskrit, meaning "a place where one strives to attain a goal in a disciplined manner". I joined about a thousand pilgrims in an evening session of meditation. Most people had their eyes closed as the inevitable sound of "OM" rippled through the air. My eyes opened from time to time. I was observing again as opposed to joining in. Was this part of the issue? I gave into temptation and suddenly fell under a wave of cynicism. This ashram with its guaranteed staple diet of devoted pilgrims. Money. Personality cult. While they were all trying to focus on universal spirit and love, I was thinking of Waco, Branch-Davidians, the Church of Scientology, Tom Cruise. This is not an episode I am proud of, and demonstrates a base instinct all too common in some so-called "investigative journalists". A recourse to base motives rooted in a corrosive cynicism.

Since taking leave of this famous guru in June 2005 I have followed any news of him with considerable attention to detail. He is the genuine article. The awards and tributes to his peace efforts run to pages and pages. You would practically need a telephone directory to accommodate it all. He has mediated between Muslims and Hindus over the thorny problem of the holy site at Ayodha in Uttar Pradesh and, most notably, was instrumental in the path to peace in Colombia in 2017 as the FARC (the self-named "Revolutionary Armed Forces of Colombia") handed in its weapons and transitioned towards being a legitimate, non-violent political party in the country's democratic system. This breakthrough ended decades of brutal kidnappings, drug trafficking and terrorist tactics which had plagued the Colombian population. Maybe you cannot measure the ocean with a spoon, but rare are the individuals on this planet who can lay claim to such achievements.

Our time in India was drawing to a close. However, just as we had found a small oasis of Catholic inspiration in Indonesia in that encounter with Father Fernando, I sought a similar venture here before we traveled on to Thailand. Hindus and Muslims account for more than 90 percent of religious practice in India, and the Christian population registers barely 3 percent. Neelima came up with a brainwave. She had heard of a church on the coastline of Tamil Nadu that had opened its doors to hundreds of flee-ing locals when the enormous tsunami wave had emerged from nowhere on that Boxing Day morning. The church was situated three hundred and fifty kilometers south of Chennai in a small town called Velankanni on the Coromandel coast in the Bay of Bengal.

Why was there a church there at all? Folklore has it that in the six-teenth century a group of Portuguese sailors were in mortal danger several miles out to sea during a violent tempest. In the Catholic tradition, the Virgin Mary is known as "Stella Maris", the star of the sea, and the desper-ate crew threw themselves upon the mother of God in their hour of peril. The one hundred and seventy men on board made a pledge. If their vessel could somehow be saved and brought to safety, the sailors would construct a basilica to her in honor of her memory. As if that narrative of the calming of the seas were not enough, locals were also inspired by accounts of the ap-parition of the Virgin to a local shepherd boy and the miraculous healing of a buttermilk vendor. None of these tales is documented in written records. They have all been passed on by oral tradition. The shrine erected to her is called "Our Lady of Good Health" and every September some five million pilgrims flock to the site for nine days of festival and prayer.

As our vehicle drew up on the coast, the resplendent white gothic structure loomed about a mile away straight ahead. It was perched on raised ground, and so the reports of scores of local Tamils fleeing the gi-gantic waves back in 2004 all made a great deal of logistical sense. These panic-stricken individuals would have thrown themselves at the mercy of the mother of God as they clambered into the church precincts and high to safety. We parked our vehicle and marveled at the sight of dozens of the devoted faithful inching along in the sand on their knees, meter by meter, slowly towards the shrine ahead.

Neelima had secured an encounter with the rector of the basilica, Father Xavier. As we wandered into the inner courtyard of the shrine-com-plex we saw an almighty line of people. It snaked all the way down from the upper floor balcony terrace, down the stairwells and across a yard. There must have been eighty to a hundred visitors all told.

"What are they queuing for?" I asked Neelima. Subbu, the only one among us with confident Tamil communication skills, made some enquiries.

"They are all waiting to see rector," came the reply. This made me slightly concerned. Our schedule for this last full day was pretty choc-a-bloc and I didn't fancy a three-hour wait. But no fears, the magic cry of "BBC" went up and, like a hot knife through butter, we by-passed the crowds and found ourselves in the rector's office.

"You're in big demand!" I exclaimed to him as we exchanged greetings. This was a tall and gentle-looking man, shrouded in a one-piece white gown or cassock. "What do all these people want from you?" I enquired.

"Many, many things," he answered. "Some want letters of approval for school places, some want medicines or referrals for the hospital, and yet more need charity donations of food or clothes for their family. This may be a religious shrine, but in truth, we handle every type of inquiry under the sun here."

I looked at the faces staring from outside into the office and felt my eyes welling up with tears. The look of reverence and esteem with which these men and women held our interviewee was really quite something. What was it I had said to Richard Dawkins in his Oxford home before we departed? *"I'd say I have met, in my lifetime, a very small number of people who exude what I would call 'a peace that surpasseth all understanding.' They have a sense of great calm and holiness about them and that always seems to be rooted in a profound sense of the sacred."* Even though I had been in his presence barely a matter of minutes, there was something transcendental about this man; his manner of talking, the way he glided effortlessly around, his radiant smile and the look of his golden-brown skin next to that pristine white garment. You honestly felt in the presence of some force of energy bigger, so much bigger, than what the human senses detected.

The events of December 26, 2004 had been unforgettable for Father Xavier and his parish team. Consoling as it was that the shrine's elevated position acted as a refuge magnet for the scampering hordes, what was etched firmly in his mind was the memory of going outside after the wave had receded.

"I went outside and, at first, I didn't see very much water, so I was struggling to comprehend the size of the tsunami wave," he said. "But after ten minutes I began to see them. All the bodies floating this way and that. Only then could I begin to imagine what calamity had taken place. But I was not shaken. I entrusted everything to our Blessed Mother."

Had he, I wanted to know, been inundated with people in the days following, posing questions about the goodness of God and how he could have let this happen?

"No, it was only people like you, media persons who came here and asked these questions," he said, with a glint in his eye and a knowing look. "The people who underwent all that, they are religious. They come to all this with a resigned heart." Implying, in his carefully chosen words, that my very question betrayed the fact that I was not "resigned". How right he was. A blunt question followed.

"Why has God made a world which features earthquakes and natural disasters?" I said, slightly raising my voice and with a touch of firmness that had not featured previously. He looked back at me and let out the faintest of sighs.

"I see you want to make everything perfect from your viewpoint," he replied. That knowing smile had returned. "But the suffering of such calamities is not the end of everything for Him." We were back to Job. "It's all much bigger than you realize. Do you know how hard it is being God?"

For a moment my mind flipped back to, of all people, the Hollywood actor, Morgan Freeman. In the wonderfully entertaining 2003 film, *Bruce Almighty*, Freeman, cast as God in his white suit, holds an encounter with the hapless failing TV journalist, Bruce (Jim Carrey). Bruce has lost his job, is in relationship meltdown with his girlfriend, and in a moment of angry supplication, cries out to God to fix it all. He is invited to meet his maker, and Freeman coolly tells him that it isn't as easy as he thinks being the Almighty. He gives Bruce all His powers for a week. The only thing he cannot do is interfere with human free will. The journalist initially engages in childish pranks, dividing a bowl of tomato soup à la Moses, and scrambling the speech of his arch work enemy, Evan Baxter, whilst his ex-colleague is live on air. The newscast becomes a cascading Tower of Babble. But then the flippancies give way to seriousness. Bruce is inundated with siren voices in his ear. The petitions of the world's faithful drown him out. He miraculously converts their prayers to emails via a computer program. Within an hour or two he has 1,527,503 unanswered requests for assistance. He despairs at the overload and on his hastily downloaded "Yahweh Insta-Prayer" facility, he sets up an "answer 'yes' to all" response. Within twenty-four hours there are riots all over the United States. Millions of people have won the lottery and the winning prize is a mere handful of cents as the share of the winning cake is a mere pittance. It sure ain't easy being God. Especially when the thing you want more than anything in the world is to repair your relationship with your nearest and dearest. Bruce, due to the restrictions on interfering with human self-determination, cannot compel his girlfriend to love him by simple fiat. God's powers are of no use. He must find other ways to repair the fractured love affair.

Father Xavier's words, "I see you want to make everything perfect from your point of view," I had taken as a mild rebuke. Here was a man, supremely secure in his faith, who was evidently *not* especially pressed to make everything perfect from *his* point of view. Why was he content to just leave it unanswered whilst I was still thrashing around trying to make sense of it all? As we ended our interview, I caught him, briefly staring out the window from his study to the scenes in the courtyard below where the throngs of people awaited an appointment. Maybe deep down he did have misgivings, a restlessness, and a sense of ennui, but I sure as hell couldn't detect it. The sense of supreme composure extended to everything he did. When we walked, he appeared not to take separate jerky steps, but to al-most glide along the tiled floor. I had never come across anything like it in my life and was overcome with not a little envy. I wanted what he had, a resolute profound faith that was so solid, so anchored, that these questions that gnawed away at me would just be swatted off as minor irritants rather than something that threatened the basis of the whole project.

When we stepped out of his study and outside onto the first-floor bal-cony, we saw that the sea of anxious faces of the local poor and needy had doubled in number. He wanted to accompany us down to the main gate and say his farewells, so we all now walked the gauntlet past a stream of hundreds of expectant people. And the way they looked at him. Non-stop expressions of deference, of utmost respect. Many thrust out their hands to touch his garment as he passed and then made a sign of the cross after they had retracted their limbs. It was as though God was walking in their midst. From nowhere, tears began to well up. From time to time, he stopped to talk, to engage them. It was never a haughty, patronizing exchange. And in return they clasped their hands together in the hope that, when he returned, he would remedy whatever problem they had. When I saw their faces, the waterworks went into overdrive and, out of embarrassment, I purposely held back and separated myself from the rest of the team. Some of the locals had seen that I had been moved to tears and looked on quizzically. Finding a discreet alcove before we descended to the ground floor, I took a brief moment to wipe them away and compose myself.

Father Xavier took us to the edges of the shrine's precinct and from the front gates we recorded a short sequence in which he showed us how far the tsunami water had reached, where the rushing masses had stampeded into the church grounds and climbed up the steps, higher and higher to safety. The less fortunate had not made it. It was their corpses that he had discovered closer to the coastline in the aftermath. At our farewell handshake, I felt the tears returning. There was now so much I wanted to say to him, but it would have all been emotional babble. I limited it to "God bless you and all the work you do here with these people". He smiled and gave that characteristic sideways Indian headshake of affirmation.

"And blessings on you and your team too," he replied. "I hope you find some answers to your questions. I will hold you in my prayers."

And with that he turned from us and went back into the shrine of Our Lady of Good Health to start attending to the needs and demands of his faithful.

"Are you OK?" asked my perceptive cameraman. Bruno had clocked the tears. Not surprising really, as he had registered them the last time, on the back of that truck as we had meandered around the carnage of Banda Aceh in Sumatra ten days ago.

"Yes, yes," I replied. "But I need to compose my thoughts. Something of great significance happened back there with Father Xavier. I'm still trying to work out what it was and if there's anything I can say about it." I asked him to have the camera ready to record. Five minutes later, I took up my position down on the beach where the tsunami wave had roared in. I was wearing the one-dollar shirt that Fauzan had bequeathed me in Sumatra. I now stared into the camera lens and said the following:

"Some of these individuals with their faith, and it's so much stronger than the faith I have, there's something at the core of who they are that doesn't get communicated by the words, the things that they say. They emanate a presence which is so much more powerful than mere words. And I'm—I'm just beginning to understand that the intellect really does have its limits. It has its role, but my goodness, it has its limits."

Scores of curious onlookers gathered around us as we, in typical fashion, needed three or four "takes" to master the recording. What is noticeable now, looking back at the film, are the tears that well up and break forth as these words about "the limits of the intellect" are shared with the audience. What had moved me so profoundly was not just the way Father Xavier had batted off my questions with such grace and nonchalance, it was something deeper. My questions had all been framed in a fairly aggressive inquisitorial fashion. And, strictly speaking, he had not answered them on my terms. But, I thought more and more to myself, "his whole life is an answer to the question". Maybe the most adequate response to the vexed quandaries of undeserved suffering was a life dedicated to those who suffer. If grieving parents were in pieces at the loss of their four-year-old child due to leukemia, you wouldn't start giving them lectures on natural selection, inadequate genes being removed from the pool and the betterment of the stock of human genetics. You would, I hope, place your hand in theirs, hug them, and . . . say nothing.

The German philosopher Martin Heidegger wrote frequently about *Dasein*.[8] This concept has been rather lazily translated in some circles as "existence", but this is a weak and rather lame attempt. Fuller accounts render it as "Being-in-the-World", that is to say, human mind and spirit are fashioned and shaped by their lives concretely lived. One's actions and efforts in the material world have a profound effect on our very way of thinking, existing, and on our spirit. This interacting with the environment is not just about "doing good works" and living well. It is deeper. It can reach profoundly inwards and transform the soul. I believe in my heart of hearts that that is what I encountered in my meeting with Father Xavier. His "answer" to my persistent questions was not a formula of words. It was his very life—a life supremely well-lived.

This was a fitting place to stop and take stock of our time in India. I felt as though I had crammed a lifetime into eight days of experience. It had been sensory overload. The spiced food, the endless colors of the procession of Hindu gods and goddesses at scores of temples, some ornate and grandiose, others a modest impromptu shack on the corner of a road barely perceived through the scented emissions of joss sticks. After the bleak austerity of our time in Indonesia, this had been a dizzying kaleidoscope which had stimulated both body and soul. But despite their huge differences, Indonesia and India had been united in one profound respect: the presence of tears at the end of the respective journeys. An insight that gave me much food for thought as we packed those bags, renewed our acquaintance with those all too familiar silver equipment boxes, and headed off to the airport.

Destination Thailand. And my first ever encounter with the wisdom of Buddhist monks.

---

8. The notion of "Dasein" is most fully explained in Heidegger's seminal 1927 work, *Sein Und Zeit* (Being and Time).

4

Thailand

Where Buddhism Tells Me "Death Is My Friend."

FOR MOST OF MY life, I have harbored a terror of dying by drowning. The thought of being consumed and vanquished by a tsunami wave constitutes my Orwellian "Room 101". As tales of Covid-19 patients gasping for air have filled our newspapers since the early months of 2020, I have striven and failed to banish from my mind the genuine horror of the thought of my lungs filling up with water. I have read in several articles that if that happens, once you stop fighting and accept your mortal fate, then the experience can actually be quite liberating, pleasant almost. Just who are the people returning from the dead to give us this precious and unexpected testimony I ask myself?

For me, this is not totally irrational. It is a profound terror based firmly on human memory. Aged six, I was left with my older brother Christopher during the summer holidays of 1965. Mother was at work in her shop, Dad was on the buses and my elder sibling, now aged eleven, was in loco parentis and trusted enough to take me to the local swimming baths. I'd proudly packed my new shiny blue and red trunks and rolled up my black and white towel and placed them all snugly in my duffel bag. I don't know where it came from, maybe newspaper photos of swimmers at the 1964 Tokyo Olympics, but I automatically assumed I could swim without the slightest bit of tuition. Christopher was taking his time getting changed in our cubicle and I was eager to get going. Without his noticing, I skipped out the door and briefly showered before following a gang of young lads through the impressive swing doors and into the main pool area.

I was, at once, knocked back by the piercing acoustic din of the sharp screams of youngsters in the water below. I didn't register the presence of shallow and deep sections of the pool. I simply charged forth and dove in with gay abandon. What a terrible move. I had, unwittingly, launched myself into the eight feet deep end. I imitated swimming strokes, but only succeeded in thrashing around with my head in and out of the water. My eyes were stinging because of the chlorine. I swallowed copious mouthfuls of the treated water. It was poison. All told, I was probably only in the pool for twenty or thirty seconds at most, but it seemed an eternity. I was eventually fished out by an attentive lifeguard and laid out face down on the tiled area at the side of the pool. A group of onlookers gathered around. After some time, the anxious figure of my brother finally emerged through the cordon of spectators. He duly got an earful from the swimming pool attendant for letting me escape his supervisory attention. My sinuses ached with the pungent odor of chlorine for hours.

On the way home, I pledged to my brother not to say a word of what had happened in the pool once we got back into the company of our parents. From that point on, my mum and dad never really did fully understand why I never took to swimming and why I would, from 1965, avoid every invitation to submerge myself in water. Nine years later, during a chemistry lesson in which we were preparing chlorine in the science labs, I got a strong whiff of the stuff and was horrified to register that my muscles were tensing up. I was in the early stages of some form of seizure or panic attack. I promptly made my excuses to the teacher and fled the scene. To this day I cannot bear the sight and sound of indoor chlorinated swimming pools. The open sea with crashing waves is another matter, as long as I don't get out of my depth. It carries less traumatic association. In social situations I still dread, in new company with those who do not know my past, the embarrassment of admitting that I never learned to swim. It's akin to the recovering alcoholic who suddenly becomes the focus of curiosity for declining that glass or two of chilled sauvignon blanc and blurts out some reason as to why drink doesn't really agree with them instead of fessing up to the truth. Many is the time that I have declined to take the plunge without going into a full explanation for my distinct lack of appetite for matters aquatic.

Against this backdrop of childhood trauma, how very odd it was to find myself on our next stop after India, strolling down the streets of Bangkok and placing myself in the line of fire of huge water cannons. This was Thai New Year and the feast of *Songkran*, the Khmer National Holiday. The two-day-long water festival is central to everything. Temperatures hit ninety degrees Fahrenheit. It is horrendously humid and so, getting doused with water from a team of total strangers is, if anything, a welcome development, even to a total aquaphobe like myself. Water fights break out everywhere as far as the eye can see. Vehicles draw up alongside you on the sidewalk, and, out of nothing, a gang of total *inconnus* fling open the passenger doors and start firing at you with water pistols. For the most part, it's gentle fun and, as a follow-up, one's assailants will then often approach and caress your face with a moist chalky paste on both cheeks, a gesture of good luck for the year ahead.

Why all this emphasis on water? Because throughout the whole of this region, from Singapore, up to Cambodia, Vietnam, Burma, and Laos, the old passing year has to be forgotten, the slate wiped clean in preparation for the year ahead. *Songkran* is derived from the Sanskrit word *Sankranti*, which means "transmigration of the Sun". April is the month of Aries, the first sign in the astrological cycle. In short, this is a festival of new beginnings and fresh starts. As we wandered the streets, we witnessed crowds pouring into Buddhist temples and splashing buckets of water all over statues of the Buddha. Monks in swirling orange robes emerged onto the streets and extended their palms to receive their blessings from the crowds. I could make sense of all this. I'm a Catholic after all, and grew up with holy water in plastic receptacles of the Virgin Mary all around the parental home. Indeed, one of my earliest conscious memories, aged three, was being soaked by an overly enthusiastic cleric who aimed his water dispenser right at my face during the blessing of our palms a week before Easter as we commemorated the triumphal march of Jesus into Jerusalem on a donkey.

"Mummy, mummy, Jesus has wet me," I am alleged to have screamed, much to the hilarity of the packed congregation at St Mark's parish church. That was all before I thought I was an Olympic gold medalist swimmer three years later, with all of its life-changing consequences.

We captured the best scenes from *Songkran* on camera for a specific purpose: to illustrate the utter ambiguity of water. That which blesses, irrigates, cleanses and purifies is also the instrument of death in Noah's flood, the near demise of St Peter as he sinks on the lake, and the cause of a farmer's ruin when adequate rainfall turns into torrents of excess and a whole year of agricultural profit can go to ruin in a matter of days. As with so much on this delicately poised planetary home called Earth, it is all down to fine tuning.

The Thai capital of Bangkok was just a one-night base before we headed south to the tourist resort of Khao Lak on the Andaman seaboard. This, along with Phuket, lay about five hundred kilometers directly east of the epicenter of the earthquake on December 26 which had precipitated the huge tsunami waves. Four and a half thousand people, many of them western vacationers, had been victims of the disaster. One man who had escaped miraculously with his life is the current President of Finland, Sauli Väinämö Niinistö. It is hard to imagine the scene, but as the water swept in, he grabbed his two young sons and ascended a huge streetlamp off the highway, somehow managing to keep himself and his children out of reach of the water for hours on end until rescuers mercifully came to his assistance.

Media reports in the west of the tsunami disaster and its aftermath had been hugely shaped by narratives of the travails of hapless tourists being caught up in countless Christmas holiday nightmares. These tales were often close to home. My late dear friend from the BBC, Sarah Hann, was beside herself with anxiety on account of her father, John, who had flown off for some mid-winter sun to Sri Lanka. He had installed himself in a coastal chalet very close to Galle in the south of the island. Having completed his morning breakfast, he was in the midst of packing his suitcase prior to departure. An unexpected visitor crashed through the door. A tsunami wave that hadn't been even polite enough to knock. Poor Sarah and the Hann family went more than four days with her father completely incommunicado. He had insisted on travelling alone and, for a man in his eighties, he was still fiercely independent and had the energy for international travel. In spite of that, the family had assumed the worst. Then, out of the blue, they received a call from the British authorities. Eighty-three-year-old John Hann had been located and transported to a military air base in Belgium. Could Sarah make it out to meet him and accompany him back to the UK? Some days later, with the balm of relief still soothing her psyche, she told me what had happened.

"He found himself floating inside his room and gasping for breath," she said. "He managed to swim out through the doorway, out of his chalet and had somehow clambered to safety."

"Was he hurt at all?" I asked her. "No fractures, bruises, concussion?" A pause on the phone.

"No duckie. He's a strong swimmer. The only serious casualty were his false teeth. He had them in a glass on the bedside table and now they are floating adrift somewhere in the Indian Ocean." Two factors had saved him. He really was an excellent swimmer and, in the tsunami's aftermath, he had been gathered up and cared for by a local hotelier, along with a host of other survivors. The air force plane had repatriated dozens of fortunate men, women, and children of many nationalities back to Europe. However, all this elderly survivor had left to wear was a t-shirt, shorts, and a pair of sandals. A kindly solider had donated a pair of socks on board and, mercifully, thrown him a blanket. It's numbingly cold up at thirty-five thousand feet. Especially when the mode of transport is airborne for the best part of twelve hours. I can't imagine there was cabin service, in-flight movies, and a glass of bubbly on offer.

As the dentureless John Hann had been swimming to safety, more than a thousand miles east at the Kamala Temple north of Phuket, an elderly lady, Manee Kuanoon, was preparing to bestow an offering to the local monks. The normally sanguine and unflappable Buddhist community was becoming inexplicably agitated.

"They starting shouting at the tops of their voices, water is coming, water is coming," she told me. We were sitting in the very place where she had been caught off guard in the temple precinct. "The water was coming in so fast. There is no way we could run away from it. I thought, where am I supposed to go?" She was effectively trapped as she could see nowhere to gain access to higher ground, and she now had a matter of seconds before the wave would implode inside the temple courtyard and sweep her away. However, her fate was to lie, literally, in others' hands. The temple abbot, Phra Kunsawad, had Manee in his sights.

"It was my pure instinct that day just to protect myself and run away," he said, brimming up with emotion as he recalled the mere seconds he had to make a decisive choice. "Then I saw this woman. It was Manee. And I knew that if I didn't turn back and try and reach her, it would be a sin and it would stay with me forever." Manee recalls all too well what happened next.

"There was this monk. He was calling out, 'Hold on to my robe, hold on to my robe.' But no matter what I did, I couldn't lever myself up." The water was now gushing in at an alarming rate. It was a question of now or never. Whether Manee lived or perished would be decided by what happened in the next few seconds. "I thought of a higher power," she said. "I made one final effort. I grasped his robe and just forced myself up." Through sheer willpower, the Abbot yanked the old lady up to a platform to safety high in the temple complex. He, along with the other monks, also managed to save many other lives that day.

Manee had not seen the Abbot since the day of her remarkable escape. For the purposes of relating their story, we now brought them together in the very area of the temple grounds where the events of her dramatic escape had unfolded. In a most deferential manner, she sat at his feet as he occupied an elevated position on the raised platform in front of her and she offered him food, flowers, and some incense. Hands were clasped together in supplication. Tears rolled down her face and she gave thanks. It was an incredibly touching scene, one made all the more authentic by the fact that the hero of the story was not used to such attention. The Abbot looked on in a manner that suggested he was mildly embarrassed by all this show of gratitude. But the more he tried to downplay it all, the more that Manee piled on the praise and recognition.

A little while later, I sat down with the Abbot to ask him a few "bigger picture" questions. What sense was there, if any at all, in events like the tsunami and the suffering that goes along with it?

"Some people were from abroad," he said. "So why did they die here together? Perhaps in the last life they were all from the same tribe. They maybe did something bad together and now they are being punished as a result of bad karma."

I found this shocking. I had somehow expected a learned monk not to take recourse to the "K" word (naïve and, retrospectively, rather patronizing of me I now concede. After all, karma had been a predominant cultural concept in these parts for centuries, so why would he be somehow free of its influence?). It seems that nobody was capable of a "wrong place at the wrong time" explanation. Everything had to be assimilated into some systemic explanation, some grand scheme. Yet on further reflection after this encounter, I realized that deep down, this "explanation" wasn't particularly adequate for me either. An existence of chance happenings, random events with no ultimate purpose, pattern and coherence may have its defenders as a *Weltanschauung*, but it was not a place I especially wanted to go. Why was I resisting the "life as patternless chaos" option? Purely because it made me "uncomfortable"? If so, from where did such dissonance emanate? An irrational loyalty to my own "tribe" and a fear of betraying parents and childhood memories? I am sure that was at least some modest part of it. But I still clung on to a conviction that there was more to all this than I had so far learnt. Where was this taking me? Into a renewal and deepening of a sophisticated and three-dimensional faith or into an honest, no holds barred cul-de-sac of the dreaded nihilistic black hole?

Such self-conscious soul-searching often came in the wee small hours of the night. On our jam-packed filming schedule there was simply no time on most days for the luxury of a Hamlet-style deliberation. Maps had to be read, locations discovered, and interview questions planned. I was plotting out more questions now for our next encounter just up the coast at Khao Lak. The third of our splendid location researchers, Jum Suppatra, had come across the story of a young woman named Wanlapha. Unlike Manee's tale of extraordinary rescue, I was warned in advance that this tale did not have a happy ending. We met up on the site of her old house right by the beach and, after some brief introductions, our director of photography, Bruno, filmed a short scene of Wanlapha and myself strolling around on the shore. She took me over to a huge palm tree and pointed up to a very large plant pot which had been lodged high, high up in its branches some fifteen to twenty feet above the sand.

"That was in my house," she said. "Before it was swept away." She pointed out some pieces of cement and rock, the sole remains of what had been the family abode. Until December 26, 2004.

On the day in question, Wanlapha had been up early and off to work at a hotel someway inland from her home. When the wave crashed onto the coastline, she ran as fast as she could to alert her two daughters, ten-year-old Orawa and five-year-old Orapan who she had left behind under the supervision of her brother.

"I tried phoning them but all the lines were blocked," she told me, holding up an imaginary mobile phone to her ear. "The threat of the water made it impossible to get anywhere near, so I turned round and made for the hills." I thought I detected a wholly understandable look of maternal guilt on her face. She had wanted to return to the house, but a second wave swept in. She had to stay put on higher ground with her husband. All night she telephoned. All night the same negative result. "I was praying everything was all right and next morning, the waters had receded, and we sped down to the house," she told me. "Everything was destroyed."

Now homeless, Wanlapha went into overdrive in a desperate search for her missing children. "We made a tour of all the temples but we had no luck. Then after five days of looking everywhere and hardly sleeping, we finally found the little one [Orapan]. I recognized her from a photo. Not by her face, but because of her bangle and necklace." I was speaking to her some five months after the event. Up to this point, there had still been no trace of her elder daughter, Orawa. Wanlapha became so upset during our interview that we had to suspend our chat and allow her some time to recompose herself.

"Why did this happen to us?" she said, looking up to the sky. I kind of sensed what was coming next. "Maybe my kids, they committed bad sins in their previous lives and they are now paying the price." I was now getting used to the karmic mantra and was sounding less and less indignant every time I voiced my reaction to it. I told her that this really sounded strange to a westerner such as myself, as a rooted conviction in reincarnation was alien to so much of our thinking. But she simply stared at me and shrugged her shoulders. "If I don't look at it like this, I won't be able to deal with it and let go," she informed me.

When our interview came to an end, Bruno switched off the camera and we just sat there for what seemed like an eternity. Some silences are comfortable. But they are normally the fruit of years of easy friendship and companionship. This was not that place. After she had wiped away more tears, Wanlapha fixed her gaze on me, and it prompted me to blurt out more words.

"Do you think you've ruled out being a parent forever? I mean, you are young, in your late twenties. Surely it's not too late?" However well intentioned, this question could easily have come across as suggesting that her children could just simply be replaced in a straightforward act of human reproduction. I cringed as soon as I said the words. But there was nothing straightforward about the suggestion.

"I can't," she said, her face creasing up in anguish. "I have had . . . what do you call it, ectopic pregnancies which means there is only one course of action open to me: IVF [in-vitro fertilization]. It's about five thousand dollars for every round of treatment at the clinic." She looked around at the now vacant site where her house once stood. "I mean, I don't even have anywhere to live and raise any children. How could I get IVF? We don't have any money."

The next few words I probably shouldn't have uttered. But I did. I leant forward, put my hand on hers and said: "We'll get you the money." There was the inevitable time delay for translation as Wanlapha looked up to Jum, our local producer, to make some sense of what had been said to her. She could tell straight away that what I had said was a tad controversial, judging from my colleague Charlie's immediate reaction. He jumped straight in and said in whispered tones into my right ear:

"You can't say that, Mark. You can't raise her hopes." Once Wanlapha had comprehended what I had said, we had more tears and a certain awkwardness which passed between us. But that was how we left it. "We will get you the money." I heard myself saying it time and again in the ensuing days. As a film crew we subsequently had long discussions about the initiative, which begged all sorts of moral and ethical questions. Did we have a role, as journalists, to assist people whose plights we featured in our productions? If we did, how did we decide who to help and to what extent, given the fact that you couldn't help everyone? Was it operationally easier just to have a simple blanket "no" to requests for help or making spontaneous offers of assistance? There was certainly an issue with keeping in touch with individuals once you had filmed them. By the time we embarked on our *Tsunami: Where Was God?* film, I had been in the trade for some twenty years and had acquired quite a backlog of interviewees, many of whom fell into the category of "deserving causes". Could one really take all that on?

These are knotty questions and journalists will answer them in a variety of ways. What would have been unforgiveable would have been to make a pledge of financial support and then simply fail to act on it. When the completed documentary was transmitted in December 2005, I enlisted the help of the nearby Anglican Church in London, St Bride's in Fleet Street, fittingly known as "the journalists' church". Whenever reporters are killed, injured, or taken hostage, large crowds would gather here in prayer and commemoration. The rector, the Reverend David Meara, circulated an appeal on Wanlapha's behalf with all the program details on some specially prepared transmission cards. I did the same among my cohort of friends and contacts, and by the end of January 2006 we had raised just under seven thousand dollars. The money was wired off to Jum in Bangkok for safekeeping as we were concerned that if Wanlapha received all the money in one large instalment there would be no shortage of needy people around her who might put her under pressure to part with it and her IVF opportunity would be lost.

She began appointments at a fertility clinic with her husband in the late spring of 2006. The prospects were far from promising on account of her husband's poor sperm count, and the couple were told to be patient. All the more surprising then that Wanlapha became pregnant on the very first cycle of treatment. Some sixteen years after we filmed in Thailand, I got back in touch with Jum just to get the details of the story accurately in place.

"I have just been on the phone to discuss this again with Wanlapha," she told me. "The doctor told her that the chances of this happening were about one in a million, because of both her and her husband's condition." On March 24, 2007, she gave birth to a son. His formal name was "Wisrut", which means "famous person". Wanlapha told Jum this was the choice of a local monk, and deeply appropriate as "famous people from the TV crew gave life to him." However, as is the local custom in Thailand, an informal nickname is also bestowed on the newly born. The doctor had a suggestion. "You should call him 'Fluke'," he said. And, to this very day, he is known to friends and family alike . . . as "Fluke".

The following day, we drove up the coast, ten miles north of Khao Lak to the Buddhist temple of Wan Yat Yao. "This is going to be quite a hard day I think," said Jum. "This place was never off the TV news for days and days after the tsunami." She explained that after Boxing Day the local hospital mortuary some two miles away was almost immediately packed to the rafters with corpses. The authorities had turned to the local community of saffron-robed monks to help them out with their storage problem. Huge cargo crates were drafted in and piled high in the courtyard to house hundreds and hundreds of decaying bodies. It was estimated that around half of them were tourists who had been swept off the beach.

"The stench at that time was overpowering," said one of the younger monks, Vichit, who gave up his morning to take me on an impromptu tour of the temple. "Even two miles away in the hospital they could smell the decomposing bodies," he told me. "Honestly, this was such a hard time for us. In the temple we are supposed to meditate and practice discipline of the mind, but every time you closed your eyes and tried to detach yourself, this odor would just come back and completely take over."

In this community of monks, Vichit was certainly one of the younger members. Ages are hard to fathom when heads are shaved, but my guess was that he was perhaps in his late twenties or early thirties and had never been exposed to death before, at least never on this scale.

"Come with me," he said. "I will show you something very interesting."

We grabbed the camera and tripod and he marched us over to a large building. It looked like a kind of depot, hall, or maybe a large community center. He opened up the creaky external doors and we followed him in.

Initially we were in near darkness, but with a quick flick of the wrist he found the lights. What a shock. What a terrible gallery of death. Peeling away, row by row in front of us, were hundreds and hundreds of photos of the tsunami deceased. They stretched out the length of six or seven distinct avenues.

"Here I will leave you to look and take some pictures," he said. "And when I come back we can talk about death." Right. Beats an inane superficial chat about the price of sugar I guess.

For the days that followed, I always referred to this place as "The Death Museum" with members of the production team. For indeed, the whole set-up was that of an art gallery. The macabre framing of the pictures and the distinct aisles that separated all the images. One almost expected a curator or a museum attendant perched on a wooden chair making sure you didn't get too near the exhibits. Alas there were no such restraints on our viewing, and we were able to get right up close. Within seconds my mind went back to that scene, months earlier, where I had to identify my father after his three weeks in Spain following his sudden demise. The destructive wave was like a huge net that had caught up all before it. It made no discrimination in its victims. Here they all were: young and old, men and women, tourists and locals. I was to learn later that this was just a small proportion of the death toll, as many of the bodies had either been washed out to sea or had been so long in the water that they had been disfigured beyond any hope of recognition.

"This is a really tricky scene to film," said Bruno. "I mean, so much of this you couldn't show on television. What time in the day is our film being transmitted?"

"Not sure," I replied. "Maybe 8 pm?" The generally agreed "watershed hour" in the UK for scenes that are considered "adult" (violence, depictions of an overtly sexual nature and general "bad taste") is 9 pm, so we were possibly on the borderline depending on how far into the documentary this particular scene would appear. Bruno concentrated on wide shots, out of focus images, and also pointed the camera at me, aiming to pick up my reaction to what I was taking in. Of course, the fact that the camera was not going in close and picking up specific details did not prevent me from being drawn in and coming face to face with the moment that death extinguishes the accumulated years of a human life. I didn't need a camera lens for this, I had my own eyes.

When it comes to corpses I don't think of myself as especially squeamish. In the summer holidays during my three years as a university student in the late 1970s, I had taken on a job as a hospital porter in Manchester. One of the more unpleasant tasks was to take a call from a ward sister in the lodge. "We've had a fatality on Ward MM1, can you get the trolley up here as soon as possible?" was an all too common request. You would arrive with your fellow porter to a bed scene with the typically shrouded curtains. The other patients would see you, a pair of Grim Reapers brandishing their magical trolley and about to perform another body vanishing trick. The trolley in question had nothing on the top surface, but it had an in-built cavity which exposed a kind of inner chamber once the top part was levered open. The visual effect that remained was that you arrived on the ward and disappeared again with nothing on the trolley. But behind the curtains, the two of you had lifted the deceased onto and then *into* the hollow space inside. You then drew back the surrounding curtains and made your exit under the all-knowing watchful eyes of the other patients who were now under no illusions where that hitherto poorly Mrs. Warburton had gone. Down to the mortuary and the ghoulish Cliff in his white coat and strangely cheerful, sunny expression. What kind of person enjoys doing that for a living? "Get the labels sorted out and put her in the third fridge," he'd say as though we were stocking supermarket shelves with packets of Jello. "There's an undertaker coming in ten minutes, so can you get 'O'Riley, P.' out of number one? You'll earn yourself some coffee money." Local tradition was that the funeral directors gave out fifty pence for each body they collected, an acknowledgement of the fact that it was not the most appealing of duties at the Salford Royal Hospital.

All these memories came flooding back when faced with the human carnage of the tsunami wave that lay posted in photo after photo before me. Some expressions were really quite peaceful, faces that spoke of resignation and acceptance. But others were decidedly disturbing, as though the camera had somehow captured the essence of struggle and fight that must surely occur when the shadow of mortality has descended right upon one. The Buddha taught that *dhukka*, or suffering, always emanated from an unhealthy sense of craving, of wanting to hold on to or possess things. It wasn't just material objects. If you were driven by ambition, by desire for power, for sex, for fame or notoriety then this could easily be classed as being trapped in *dhukka*. And yes, this even extended into clinging onto your very own physical existence.

Half an hour in the "gallery of death" was about as much as I could take. When I re-emerged into the sunlight of the temple courtyard, my young monk was waiting for me. He had a vaguely expectant, near mischievous look on his face. His saffron robes twirled around in the late morning breeze. "I can offer you all coffee now," he said.

"Excellent," I replied. "Just what we all need after that experience. Will you join us?" A knowing smile and a deft shake of the head.

"I will happily join you for our conversation about death," he said. "But coffee is bad for one, spiritually speaking. Too much stimulant." I felt put in my place and then gave in to another bout of caffeine-induced *dhukka*.

As we sat chatting, I shared with Vichit my reaction to the images I had just seen, especially the torment and anguish on some of the faces as they fought to the very last. He was patient and listened attentively before composing himself.

"Death is your best friend," he said, in a not very reassuring way. "Death is your closest relative. He is a companion who will never leave you."

The more my face creased up in puzzlement, the warmer and wider the smile that erupted on his face. I sensed he, more than a little, liked the shock value of his pronouncements.

"So, my friend. An honest answer to a direct question," I said. "Are you not frightened, even ever so slightly, of death?"

A sideways shake of the head. "I'm not afraid of death. The only thing I'm afraid of is my own mind," he replied. At this point he stopped smiling and suddenly looked serious. Eye contact momentarily ceased as he broke his gaze and looked away at the ground. "Do you practice yoga and meditation?" he asked. I told him about our concept of prayer, possibly the closest thing to what he was referring to. "Come," he said. "We will spend some time in temple."

As we weren't in the usual immediate hurry to get to the next filming location, I allowed myself to be led into the temple, and here we passed the best part of an hour in total silence. Birdsong and vehicle traffic made for unlikely acoustic bed partners. Rather typically, as my mind wandered, I found myself looking at the other monks and recalled what I had read about the Buddha. His sitting position, *asana*, was the precursor to *prananyama*, the art of breathing progressively more and more slowly which, after much practice, may lead to *jhana*, a near trance induced by yogic practice. *Ayatana* was the goal, "nothingness", a mental and spiritual state in which one was free of all constraints, and suffering (*dhukka*) had been eliminated. Such goals may take months, if not years to achieve, I was informed by Vichit. Indeed, many monks can spend a whole lifetime in pursuit of such objectives and these spiritual destinations will remain elusive. Some will go to their graves after decades of aspiring to this state of release and transcendence, not having tasted the fruits of vanquishing the ego and disciplining the mind. For my own part, I tried to "Christianize" this narrative and speculate about the lives of the great saints whose work was so grounded in a sense of God's mission and purpose that much of their ego had perhaps been largely banished. "For whoever wishes to save his life shall lose it; but whoever loses his life for my sake shall find it," says Jesus in St Matthew's Gospel.[1] After fifty minutes in the temple, my all too familiar noisy mind returned to filming schedules. We packed up, gave our sincere thanks, said our farewells, and put ourselves in the hands of Jum and her able driver once more.

We had previously been blessed in Indonesia with the youthful Fauzan, and in India with the supremely maternal practical arts of Neelima. Now it was Jum's turn to demonstrate just how central is the role of the location producer when making a demanding documentary such as *Tsunami: Where was God?* Jum was less demonstrative and quieter than our first two colleagues, but she had a knack of always being a step ahead. After we boarded our minibus and drove off from the Wan Yat Yao Temple, I voiced a concern with her.

"The problem with a mantra like 'Death is your friend' and all this emphasis on yoga and meditation is that we run the risk in this film of just confirming basic stereotypes," I said.

"What do you mean exactly?" she enquired.

"You know the sort of thing, that Buddhists are withdrawn from the world and above it all, rather aloof." I paused. I had never thought to ask. Was she a practicing Buddhist? Was I in danger of treading on delicate territory? "I mean, there's a lot of talk about the illusions of the world and how the mind needs to be disciplined but that's not exactly a message I'd want to hear if I had just lost my house and kids and was faced with financial ruin," I stated. Jum was now smiling. "What?" I asked. "Are we going to deal with all this at some point? What's coming up next? Where are we off to?"

The answer to that question was that we were off to another temple. To meet more monks. But here, any comparisons with Wat Yan Yao ceased immediately. A forty-minute journey up the coast and we arrived at the Samakee Temple. We had come here to see another core Buddhist principle in action. But this was to be nothing ethereal or overly metaphysical.

1. Matt 16:25.

The concept of *sila* comprises three stages on the famous eightfold noble path of the Buddha: "right speech, right action, and right livelihood."[2] Its importance is best illustrated by reference to the celebrated Buddhist parable of the poisoned arrow. Zen scholar, Philip Kapleau, summarizes the Buddha's account:

"Suppose a man is struck by a poisoned arrow and the doctor wishes to take out the arrow immediately. Suppose the man does not want the arrow removed until he knows who shot it, his age, his parents, and why he shot it. What would happen? If he were to wait until all these questions have been answered, the man might die first."[3]

In less erudite terms, you might say the moral of the tale is: "stop over-thinking it and just get on with it!" And that is precisely what the monks did at Samakee. Their neighbors at the time of the December 26 tsunami had been a community of gypsies just along the coast. They earned their living by going out in modestly constructed wooden fishing boats and trading their hauls with local bars and restaurants. On the terrible day in question, their vessels had been taken up by the huge waves and smashed to smithereens on the jagged rocks. A number of their community perished in the tragedy, but for those that survived, they returned to their fishing base days later only to find they now had no way of earning a living.

"When all this happened, we thought this temple would be a good place to come to. The monks here are a source of stability." This was community leader and master craftsman, Somchai Taosai. "They would never abandon us because they are men who are steeped in virtue," he assured me. This local fisherman had set up camp in the temple grounds with about fifty or so other people and were using the area as a recovery base for the reconstruction of their fishing fleet. Monks came and went with food and water and serviced their needs. Children ran around, gleefully playing what looked like a form of hide and seek in the hastily erected tents. When the monks walked past and smiled at them, the youngsters beamed back and often lunged forward to gently get a touch of their saffron robes. It was all a deeply uplifting sight. Just when you thought the precepts of Buddhism were all pie-in-the-sky, here was a community of devout individuals who were happy to roll up their sleeves, embrace the lessons of the parable of the poisoned arrow and get stuck in. A closer examination of the Abbot's CV would have taught me that this was hardly a surprise. Phra

2. https://www.britannica.com/topic/sila-Buddhism.

3. Hanh and Kapleau, *Zen Keys*, 42.

Suwatthithammarat had trained to be an engineer before he joined the monastery and took a very keen interest in the construction process. In his office he had constructed a miniature version of a wooden boat which had been kitted out with a tiny motorized iron rudder. After showing me this, off we went outside to examine the real thing. Workshops had been constructed. International aid had paid for the materials and an assembly line of new vessels was well under way.

"These are all what we call longtail boats," the Abbot told me with a wide, contented grin on his face. "The names of the boats are Samakee-Kla Thalae One, Two, etc. Samakee is the name of our temple and Kla Thalae is their family name. In Thai it means 'strong to go out to the sea.'"

I confessed to the Abbot that this spurt of practical virtue in action had done a lot to correct some evolving prejudices about an overly metaphysical understanding of Buddhism. Over some tea back in his office, there was a moment of serendipity. "You know the story of the poisoned arrow?" he asked. When I nodded enthusiastically, he came up with a suggestion. "You must tell this story in your film," he said. "You will need an arrow. Come."

So, after hastily finishing our tea, off we went to locate a master carpenter who was absolved from working on the boats for an hour or so and was asked to fashion us a very large wooden arrow. We did try to explain what it was for, but I think the explanation might have fallen on fallow ground. I must have cut a rather eccentric sight to the dwellers of the ad hoc fishing community and the gathering of monks who witnessed a TV reporter parading around in the precincts of the temple, holding up a very large wooden arrow to the camera and talking about the Buddha's wisdom. But we had the Abbot to thank for his inspired idea. It became a short but memorable scene in the final cut of the edited documentary.

As we finished filming for the day, what had really struck me about this tale of philanthropy and practical assistance was that, for the fishermen and their families, the temple had been the obvious place to go after disaster had befallen them. It was almost a reflex action, such was the standing of the monks and the temple in local society. It's hard to imagine a Roman Catholic bishop giving up his grounds for a nomadic group of total strangers and then rolling up his sleeves and helping out with a dose of hands-on carpentry. These people had shown faith in faith itself and it had served them well. Moreover, it was clear from observing all the comings and goings and the gentle ease between the monks and their temporary guests that this was a deeply symbiotic arrangement. The monks were pleased to be serving a purpose. It wasn't all one-way traffic.

The Samakee Temple had been an example of unconditional aid. Alas, in the grand history of intervention in disaster zones, the record is replete with examples of tales where religiously motivated proselytizers use the opportunity to offer material assistance in exchange for defection. Consider the following, published by the Freedom from Religion Foundation just a month after the tsunami struck:

> A group of Christian missionaries in the tiny Hindu village of Samanthapettai, India, reportedly refused aid if victims did not agree to convert to Christianity. The 200 starving survivors in the village, which was virtually wiped out by the tidal wave, were shocked when nuns asked them to convert before distributing biscuits and water, according to *Yahoo! India News* (Jan. 16, 2005). When missionaries saw TV reporters recording the arguments that broke out, they fled the village without unloading food, clothes, and medicine.[4]

At the same time, the International Bible Society was reported as announcing it would publish 100,000 copies of the Bible, translated into Thai, in the weeks following the Boxing Day catastrophe.[5]

The day after our visit to the boat building temple, it was, by coincidence, a Sunday, the Christian sabbath. We caught up with a group called the Mercy Foundation which was organizing an evangelical service just a few minutes' drive from where we were staying. As a TV reporter and Roman Catholic, I am never more ill at ease than when being filmed in such gatherings. The style of spirituality with all its talk of "being saved", "brother Jesus", and the like is just not how I was brought up. The thing is, if you were asked to participate in the service (and why as a fellow Christian should I decline the invitation to commemorate the Last Supper and share a eucharistic celebration?), you could always bet that the very point when the cameraman had his beady lens fixed on you was when everyone around you had their hands in the air, eyes closed and were swaying backwards and forwards. From a purely self-conscious TV image point of view ("vanity of vanities, all is vanity"[6]; how right is the author of Ecclesiastes!), you were trapped between the devil and the deep blue sea. You either joined in and

4. https://ffrf.org/news/news-releases/item/13181-tsunami-of-proselytizing.

5. https://ffrf.org/news/news-releases/item/13181-tsunami-of-proselytizing.

6. Eccl 1:2.

suffered the inward creakings of a deafening internal cognitive dissonance and the inevitable taunting of relatives and friends once the documentary went to air. Alternatively, you stood there like a frozen lemon, refusing to participate, attracting attention and possibly straining relations with the very people you were meant to be interviewing later. This "scene" repeated itself many times in my broadcasting career and I never really succeeded in developing a *modus operandi* that worked satisfactorily.

I joined the Mercy Foundation service and tried my best to cast aside self-consciousness for the best part of an hour. Our host was an American by the name of Dean Overholt. He was one of a number of westerners in the congregation who were accompanied by a couple of dozen locals. How did they end up here, I wondered, in a country where 95 percent of the population professes to be Buddhist and just 1 percent acknowledge Jesus Christ as their Lord and Savior? My suspicions were raised when I came to discover that the charity was sponsoring a house construction program. I knew of occasions in the past when relief efforts by Christian groups in time of famine and drought had offered food and water in exchange for conversion. Such converts were known as "rice Christians". When I sat down to talk to Dean, I asked him, bluntly, if that is what was going on here.

"Some people have come to us, for sure. I don't know if they'll stay," he said. "We're not forcing them to come. They listen to the scripture and the sermons. We don't pass out contracts, or documents to sign. We've been very centered, and we told the government that we are a Christian organization." He rejected the suggestion, outright, that aid was being used as a tool to proselytize and gain converts for the Lord. "I've seen other groups doing that and I think it's just tacky," he said, somewhat indignantly. "We don't do that stuff. We just don't." If we had been scheduled to be in the area for a much longer stretch of time, my natural journalistic curiosity would have driven me to do some behind the scenes digging and perhaps talk to a few of the people who were destined to take up occupation of the new accommodation. But that would have to go on the back burner as other priorities loomed before us. Suffice to say, I'd expect there to be a mixture of good and not so good practice in this area. When a certain type of Christian hears the imperative from Jesus to "go into all the world and spread the gospel to every creature",[7] he or she wouldn't see any harm in feeding or housing the poor and destitute as a stepping-stone towards saving souls.

---

7. Mark 16:15.

For myself, unconditional love means just that. There are no conditions set down. None.

Against the backdrop of all these new houses going up on the road, I wanted to ask Dean about bigger matters. How did he deal with the whole God, suffering, and natural evil dilemma? He was disarmingly frank.

"I can't make sense of it. You know . . . I mean. I just don't go there." And he stuck to his guns. I tried once or twice more in different ways, but he most definitely "did not want to go there". Yet, unlike me, it didn't seem to be presenting a major threat to the whole faith project. He had Jesus, the Lord was with him, and he seemed quite content with the fact that, in the fullness of time, all things might become clearer. What did he make of me and my continuous questioning? Perhaps a sign of my weakness and lack of resolve. There was, historically, no love lost between evangelical Baptists and Roman Catholics. Maybe my curiosity is just what you'd expect from a "Roman" with our dodgy history of supporting the Crusades, selling indulgences, the horrors of the Inquisition, and support for the corrupting tendencies of the papacy.

We took our leave of Dean, leaving the housing construction progressing ahead at full pelt. Here was a guy giving up his time, leaving his family, and spending weeks upon end trying to help the homeless. In the grand scheme of things, it was hard to be too critical.

Which is not a phrase one could extend to another faith-based intervention in the country. Amidst the research I had carried out prior to leaving the UK, a chance Google enquiry had had me stumble across the following press-release headline from a mid-western church in the heart of Kansas's corn belt: "*Thank God for the tsunamis and five thousand dead Swedes.*"[8] At first I blinked, reached for my reading glasses and brought up the sub-headline into focus. "*God is laughing, mocking and taunting Swedes even as they mourn and weep over their dead.*" What was this, some kind of spoof, a hoax? Was there really a church community called the "Westboro Baptist Church"? Further investigation took me to a number of online entries and articles on this rather bizarre community based at 3701 SW 12th St, Kansas 66604.

It was established after World War Two by a Dr Fred Phelps just west of Topeka, the Kansas State capital, and celebrated its first public service on November 27, 1955. It appeared to consist of mainly the Phelps family and friends, numbering no more than forty or fifty individuals, and has

8. Westboro Baptist Church news release, January 2, 2005.

never been affiliated with either of the two largest Baptist organizations, the Southern Baptist Convention or the Baptist World Alliance. Its internet presence is secured by its website which boasts the remarkable website address: www.godhatesfags.com. It is unapologetically homophobic in its outlook. Over the decades it has welcomed AIDS as the wrath of God against unnatural sexual practices and has even sent members to picket the funerals of young gay men whose lives have been taken in bouts of homophobic violence. Up to 2009, the Phelps family claims to have participated in more than forty-one thousand separate protests in six hundred and fifty cities. Against this backdrop, its pronouncements over the tsunami death toll seemed almost moderate, but why the rejoicing over Swedes who had gone to their deaths? Enter controversial Swedish Pastor Ake Green who, in a 2003 sermon on homosexuality, said: "The Bible clearly teaches about these abnormalities. Sexual abnormalities are a deep cancerous tumor in the entire society. The Lord knows that sexually twisted people will rape the animals."[9] Swedish courts subsequently convicted the preacher of hate speech and sentenced him to a month in prison (a verdict later overturned). So here you have it: for Westboro's Phelps family, the uncompromising Pastor Ake was an oppressed and persecuted hero. Swedish society deserved to be cursed. That is why, with five hundred and forty-three casualties, Sweden was at the top of the European death toll league table in early 2005. (Westboro Church declined to posit the proposition that, with fifteen to twenty thousand Swedes on vacation in the area, substantially more holidaymakers than any other country, it was only statistically most probable that there would be so many victims, but the narrative of a gay-hating deity hell-bent on vengeance suited its purpose rather more.)

I printed off the remarkable Westboro Church press release which rejoiced in Sweden's misery and spoke to our location producer, Jum, about it. It really did take her a few passes to digest and internalize the sheer hatred at the root of all this.

"Thailand has always been popular with visiting Swedish people," she told me. "Germans come here a lot too, but I'm not surprised there were so many casualties from Scandinavia." I pondered what we might do with this rather extraordinary outburst from Kansas. My mind was thrown back to our Aceh visit and that Islamic Defense Front spokesman who blamed the killer waves on youthful promiscuity. When natural disasters struck there

9. https://www.eaec.org/bibleanswers/ake_green_sermon.htm.

was, it seemed, never a shortage of folk around who would opportunistically aim to bend the story to their ideological ends.

Jum thought long and hard about it and, in her typically resourceful fashion, just happened to find us a Swedish citizen in Khao Lak with whom we could explore this story. If I had been taken aback by the contents of their January 2005 press release, I wondered how Bjorn Möller would react. His was a fascinating back story. Owner of a glitzy and hugely profitable restaurant in Manhattan some four hundred meters from New York's World Trade Center, Bjorn had a life-changing response to the attacks of September 11, 2001. He sold his business, flew east and had not been back to the States since. We found him in Ko Sire just outside of Phuket where he was taking a break from his day job as a diving instructor and was currently trying to raise funds to start up a kindergarten project for local orphans.

"What's all this about?" he asked, quite understandably. "Your colleague here said something about the tsunami. You know I lost several family members up the coast in Khao Lak right?"

He told me a bit about where he had been on the day in question and how he had scrambled to safety. "There's a particular Swedish angle I wanted to explore with you," I said. He looked puzzled. "I know all this sounds a bit weird, but there's a kind of 'surprise element' to it; something we have come across and I just really wanted to film your reaction to it when you see it for the first time." He still looked puzzled.

"Well, this all sounds a bit weird. But you seem nice guys. So let's just do it."

I wanted to show Bjorn the contents of the press release and then, if luck would have it, connect him by telephone to the Westboro Church in Kansas, some ten thousand miles away. It was a tricky proposal as there was a fourteen-hour time difference to take into consideration which meant we would have to schedule an interview with Bjorn in his house at about eleven in the evening (nine in the morning in Topeka, Kansas). Once we explained this to him, without giving away the telephone connection idea, he looked even more puzzled.

"Do you guys do this kind of thing all the time? It's like some TV game show," he remarked. So much of this would depend on serendipity. It had to work on the one off-chance, as our days in Thailand were coming to an end and there was a limit to how many times we could keep pitching up at Bjorn's house late at night. It all depended on chance. Would someone answer the phone at the church? Would there be a decent connection via a mobile phone ten thousand miles away? What would happen if someone just took the call and then hung up the phone? And Bjorn's reaction? He seemed a passionate kind of individual and had lost family members in December 2004. There was no second guessing how he would respond.

We gathered inside his house later that evening. I was grateful for the fact that he was clearly trusting of us all. It isn't everybody who allows a foreign film crew into the heart of his home to record for an as yet unknown objective. Once Bruno started up the camera and we were up and running, I produced the church's press release from my file and placed it in front of Bjorn.

"'Thank God for the tsunami and five thousand dead Swedes.' I mean, obviously the guy who wrote this must be living on another planet, right?" he said. He looked half confused and half enraged. "You can probably read in my eyes what I felt like doing to whoever wrote this, right?"

I told him we were going to call the people who had produced the publication. Charlie handed me a mobile phone and it seemed an age while I pushed the phone pads. This was it. Make or break time.

"Hello" said a woman at the other end.

"Is that Westboro Baptist Church?" I asked.

"Please hold for a moment." I passed the phone over to Bjorn. What follows is the entire exchange, which we broadcast, with Shirley Phelps, the daughter of Fred, the Westboro founder:

Bjorn Möller (BM): "When I say to you that some of my relatives that died here in the tsunami were children. Does this have anything to do with this thing you have about homosexuality and God?"

Shirley Phelps (SP): "All the people who died in that tsunami were sinners. But listen to this. Jesus Christ said that all the people that died in the tower at Siloam,[10] there were eighteen people who died when that tower fell. Sinners like the rest, you may say, but if you don't repent you shall likewise perish. It doesn't matter how innocent they are, they weren't doing their job."

---

10. Jesus refers to this incident in Luke 13:4–5. The tower in question was based outside the walls of Jerusalem and its collapse killed a number of nearby bystanders. Jesus makes the point that you cannot extrapolate people's sinfulness or innocence from such events. In other words, Jesus refutes the assertion that suffering is proportionate to sinfulness and that bad things only happen to bad people. Tragedy is not a sure sign of God's judgment.

BM: "OK, my relatives, OK, two children died in the tsunami, OK. From Sweden, here in Thailand. What have they done? You're saying they did something to deserve that?"

SP: "They raised them to the Devil. Because they weren't being raised in the way they should have been. How about that?"

BM: "Are you on some kind of medication? What's up with you?"

SP: "OK. Quit doing that, quit mocking me. I'm not on drugs, or whatever."

BM: "I'm not mocking you. But it seems like you guys aren't—[*at this point SP talks over him and tries to interrupt*] wait, wait, wait. It seems like you guys—I have it in print here. You are mocking people and you're mocking people that are dead, you know."

SP: "It says that God laughs and mocks when the wicked die. That's what it says. Do you want me to give you the verse?"

BM: "Yeah."

SP: "OK. Just give me a second. It's in Proverbs 1. I'm just looking on my computer."

BM: "What? You mean you don't know it by heart?"

SP: "Not this one, no."

BM: "So much hatred, you can't harbor that in your heart alone, you have to have it on the computer too? I'm sorry."

SP: "Shut up! [*Bjorn tries to interrupt*] I said shut up! You probably don't know a single verse, so, away with that. Now if you have any more questions, you can email us at godhatesfags.com."

And with that, Shirley Phelps hung up the phone and terminated one of the most bizarre telephone exchanges I have ever witnessed. The look on Bjorn's face afterwards was a picture. Dumbfounded. I am not sure that either in his native Sweden or in even in swinging Manhattan, with its reputation for brusque talking, he had ever come across anything quite so brazen and outlandish. After that, with the time approaching midnight, what we all needed was a cold beer or two. I had been more than a little apprehensive about how he would react, but he was amazingly sanguine.

"I totally accept why you did this the way you did. You had to get my authentic reaction," he quipped. "It leaves a nasty taste in my mouth for sure, but I really don't regret you pointing this out. Incredible. Absolutely incredible. As if there wasn't enough suffering going on already, these guys have to pile more of it on."

We ended up saying our goodbyes to Bjorn at something like 1 am. "I won't forget my meeting with you guys," he shouted, as we loaded up the van on the driveway outside his house. "I'm not sure I should *thank* you, exactly, but this has certainly been an encounter I won't forget in a hurry." We waved from our vehicle as it trundled off in the night.

He hadn't asked me for a contact number for the Westboro Baptist Church.

With our remaining time in Thailand running out fast, I was very mindful of the fact that I still needed to address a rather significant question: what does your average Buddhist make of "God"? As my tsunami journey had progressed, we had been initially steeped in a resolutely monotheistic Abrahamic culture in Aceh, and moved on to India where concepts of the divine were much more fluid. Yet even there, was a strong sense of the in-divisibility of *Brahman*, the so-called "Universal Principle" and cause of all that is real and exists. Some Hindus, though by no means all, are happy to equate this to what Christians call "God". But Buddhists?

Ask most lay people in the west about Buddhism and they may, if you're fortunate, know just a bit about *nirvana*. No, not the celebrated rock band, but that state of freedom from continuously recurring rebirth. The word literally means "quenching" or "blowing out" of the three fires of the poisons of sensuality, hate and ignorance. I could relate to this in some sense as "heaven", a spiritual state where all craving, restlessness, and division is banished, but as a Christian, my "heaven" made no sense without being united with the foundation of all reality and existence: God. Does a Buddhist need God? That was my question.

Not a line of enquiry to ignite your everyday conversation in the café or supermarket queue I will grant you. I spelled all this out with our local producer, Jum, and she nodded.

"Yes, I remember from your notes that you were very keen to try and answer this question with Buddhist monk," she said. "This will be our final interview." This was like Jesus at the wedding feast at Cana perhaps, leaving the best until last?

Our final interviewee awaited us at Nakhon Pathom, some thirty-five miles west of Bangkok. The Venerable Dhammananda Bhikkhuni was the community leader at the Songdhammakalyani Temple, the first temple in Thailand built by women, for women, in 1960. The Abbess was quite a fig-ure in the Buddhist world as she had become the first female in the conser-vative Theravada tradition (as distinct from the Zen school) to be ordained a monk. No male monk in Thailand would perform the ritual, and so she traveled to Sri Lanka where a willing member of a monastic community was happy to carry out the ceremony.

Female monks also shave their heads, and so my first sight of the Abbess at a distance had me somewhat confused. Was this really her or was it some male imposter?

"You are all most welcome. Before we talk, maybe I can give you a short tour of our vegetable garden?" she said in an unmistakably higher vocal register. Her lack of hair gave her an ageless appearance. Mid-forties? Mid-fifties? Hard to know. I sensed an immediate ease of presence about her, just like I had felt with that unforgettable rector, Father Xavier, at the Velankanni Basilica in Tamil Nadu.

There was no shortage of beautiful settings to choose for our interview. Shoes had been left at the temple entrance. I took special care as we squatted on the shiny floor to ensure that we were positioned well below the head level of the Buddha in front of us. (In one previous temple I had chosen to sit on some steps and was immediately ushered away by one of the local monks. When I explained to Jum what had happened she had quietly put me in my place. "It is not because you were sitting on his newly clean steps: you were elevated at head level above the Buddha. They say this is disrespectful. No one is on the same level as the Buddha.")

I got straight to the point. What sense, if any, did the venerable Abbess make of "God"?

"We are not atheists, you know. As though we would deny completely and outright that there is a God. We are rather more, *non-theist.*" There was a long pause as she watched for my reaction and whether I had digested it. "Whether God is there or not is not our main concern. If God created us, well that is all well and good. But the thing is, I am here already, so I will make the best of what I am here for." I found this gentler and more ambiguous than what I had sometimes come across among other Buddhists in the past. Some had insisted on the outright negation of the notion of "God", and even insisted that Siddhartha Gautama had decreed belief in God to be an error. But the Abbess was making a more subtle point. The existence of God, being ultimately neither provable nor unprovable by human reason and logic, represented something of a cul-de-sac. If one spent a vast swathe of one's life preoccupied by such matters, one would ultimately get nowhere and become frustrated. We were talking time opportunities. There was a real danger of navel gazing, of not using one's life to alleviate suffering. There was in fact, an echo here of the story of the poisoned arrow I had come across in the Samakee Temple. Don't ask too many impossible questions, just get on with fixing the wound!

I stayed with the gentle Abbess for quite some time, probing her with questions about the Buddhist teaching of "no self". All that western thinking of personal individual identity: Descartes' "I think therefore I am", and John Donne's "No man is an island" goes out the window when a Buddhist teaches you that what survives death is not a sense of "self" based on a unique soul, but rather a human identity, like a constantly changing mass of energy and flux: akin to a flowing river. So what happens to me when I die, I wanted to know from the Venerable Dhammananda Bhikkhuni?

"Buddhism explains it like this," she said, taking in a deep breath. "Mr. A who dies is not reborn again as Mr. A. No. Mr. B who is reborn again after Mr. A is the result, the culmination of all the actions of Mr. A. But Mr. B is not Mr. A." Got your head around that? I certainly had to think long and hard about it. In fact, the Buddha used an analogy to demonstrate the phenomenon. When you take an unlit candle and hold the wick in the center of an already glowing candle, the visual illusion is that the flame "jumps" from one to the other. But in fact, the flame in the previously unlit candle is a unique and different aggregate of energy with its own properties. It is not a mere recreation of the first flame. Everything in existence is in a constant flow of change, including human consciousness.

It was a long way from the Bible, the Catholic Catechism, and papal encyclicals. But if God exits the stage, the centuries-old theodicy contradiction of reconciling the goodness of a creator with cancer, tornadoes, Covid-19, and the like just becomes an irrelevance. So here, at the end of my journey to Thailand, was a presentable solution. I could just simply embrace Buddhism and begin my long and arduous ascent towards nirvana. (That "I" of course not being a "self" but a unique constellation of material and psychic energy in the grip of eternal flux.)

Our check-out from our hotel on our final morning didn't just mean long hugs for Jum and saying our farewells to our local Thai driver. We were now due at the airport for a very long journey home, with hours and hours of footage filmed in three countries. We had arrived in Aceh five weeks before but had packed so much in that it seemed like five years. It's a well-honed cliché to say that it was "all a blur" but it really wasn't. During that long overnight flight back to London's Heathrow airport I barely slept. I declined the opportunity to don my headphones and immerse myself in

Harry Potter and the Prisoner of Azkaban or *The Bourne Supremacy*. Instead, my mind replayed so much of what we had encountered in these five extraordinary weeks. The contrast between people who had lost their faith and those who, if anything, emerged with their belief and convictions even more intact. The polarized worlds of perfume counters in airport duty-free zones compared to the typhoid-filled shanty towns where thousands scrambled over one another in an effort to survive from day to day. Many of them relied on unprecedented international relief efforts from NGOs and their staff. And to cap it all, the militants of the Islamic Defense Front and the Westboro Church: offering no compassionate account of faith in time of human need but utilizing every last ounce of pain to advance a myopic and self-serving agenda. Job's comforters in the Old Testament had nothing on these guys.

With a couple of hours to go before we touched down, my mind turned back to practicalities. We had been commissioned to make a film of one hundred minutes. Accompanied by commercial breaks, this would effectively divide the documentary into five or six sections and cover transmission over the best part of two hours. The filming had gone well, that I knew. We had unforgettable characters and stories, some mind-bending images (such as that boat resting on top of a building on the outskirts of Aceh). In retrospect, it had gone like clockwork. None of the authorities had stopped us recording. We had next to no "no-shows" with people losing their nerve at the last minute and pulling out. But, despite the hours and hours of footage in the can, when all was edited down, how much of the final film did we currently have in our possession?

I had months to resolve this as we were due back in mid-June and, after a summer stand-down, the production was due to commence editing over a two-month schedule in the autumn in time for a delivery to Channel Four of the finalized product by late November. I would have to spend the next month logging all the footage. Timecodes, transcripts galore. But then the really tricky bit: welding all this into a compelling narrative with a beginning, a middle, and an end. Writing a script. Broadcasting is mercilessly linear I find. Unlike print, where little digressions and excursions down side-alleys are practiced by the more gifted writers, there was always something about radio and TV I found that brooked little, if any, "going off the point". It needed to be like a decorative necklace: there was no point in having all these random beautiful beads or gemstones if there was not a central thread holding it all together. We had the beginning: my father's explosive "God could have stopped that", which set up the whole question and genesis of the tsunami journey. We had the very extensive middle: the lands we had visited and the colorful, revealing encounters and what we had uncovered about different faiths and the people that practice them.

But what of the end? Would there be a definitive "conclusion" to this film? Or would I take refuge in the time-honored indecision of "it's all a mystery, but I hope you've enjoyed the ride anyhow?", the refuge of the over-prevaricating correspondent? As we began our descent from thirty-five thousand feet, the strangely comforting sight of suburban west London rooftops crystallized into view. I closed my eyes and, for once, I actually prayed for a few minutes. I don't mean prayers of supplication and petition. I simply let go and said: "shape this into what you will." To whom or what I "spoke" I know not. I may, one day. And when my fleeting moments of self-abandonment came to an end with a reminder to fasten my seatbelt, my ears "popped" and suddenly everything felt as though it was going somewhere.

I just wasn't sure where.

5

Rome and a Trip to the Vatican Observatory

WE HAD ARRIVED BACK in London in mid-June 2005 and much of the next few weeks was spent logging all the material we had shot on location. It is a very strange experience to relive all those moments when you are locked away for hours on end in a darkened room, inserting tapes in and out of viewing machines and diligently recording timecodes. Images of desperately hungry children in the rubble appeared on the monitor as I broke off another finger of KitKat and sipped rather nasty coffee from a crumbling polystyrene cup. One-line descriptions of the images were entered into a shot list, an inventory that mushroomed steadily in size as the weeks passed.

From time to time my colleagues in our compact office space in west London's Shepherd's Bush would crane their necks around the door just to get a glimpse of some of the visuals. "Oh my God, look at that," said one of them, seeing Banda Aceh's flattened landscape. "There are hardly any buildings standing. Where did everyone go?" Such outbursts were regular occurrences. As the summer gathered pace, about forty hours or more of material had been logged and I knew we had some extraordinarily powerful testimonies. However, there was nothing here so far that remotely resembled a satisfying last fifteen or twenty minutes of the film. My father had set a hare running with his "God could have stopped that" interjection. In truth, in five weeks we had amassed lots of evidence of the problem, but, barring one or two fleeting moments, very little in the way of resolution. Since his unexpected passing a few months earlier, my mother was now a widow and adjusting to the shock of being alone in a house for the first time in her life. She was seventy-six years old. I made the trip north for a long weekend to Manchester and, bit by bit, related highlights of what we had encountered. She sat there patiently and refilled our wine glasses with generous quantities of Australian shiraz. More than once she was heard to say, "what a shame your dad's not here to listen to all this." She was putting a very brave face on it, but I had a very deep conviction that this newly enforced life of solitude was not to her taste.

"Let's get the diary out and sort out a trip down on the train to London," I said.

"Ooh, that'll be nice," she said. "I've not got a lot on these days really." And looked out of the window wistfully.

The English summer of 2005 unfolded steadily with scenes a zillion light years away from the Indian Ocean. There were early evening strolls amid the lengthening shadows of Hyde Park's lime and sweet chestnut trees to take in promenade concerts of classical music at the Royal Albert Hall. Barbecues abounded in suburban gardens with an opportunity to catch up with friends I had not seen for months. I rose at 7 am on Sundays and amassed numerous terracotta pots full of color from the marvelous Columbia Road plant market on the edge of London's East End. My apartment on Fleet Street was barely two minutes from the Thames. Riverside walks, cold beers overlooking Southwark and London Bridges, and even an evening or two taking in a play at the Globe Theatre on the South Bank. All very agreeable. After what I had witnessed out east on the shores of the Indian Ocean, I counted my blessings with every passing day. But that vexed problem persisted. How to resolve the film?

Thank goodness for internet search engines. Increasingly unnerved by the incomplete nature of this tsunami journey, I was discussing what options remained open to us with Charlie in the office over a coffee.

"What we need is a sort of theodicy convention," I said, "where I can put all these questions about God and suffering in the natural world to a big gathering of believers, preferably ones versed in science and who know about such things as big bang, quantum theory, dark matter, and the like."

Charlie was encouraging. "Let's have a spurt on Google for religious cosmologists," he responded. "You never know, we just might get lucky." And so, we got down to it. Half an hour later, a "Eureka" moment.

"I don't believe it," I said, shouting to Charlie across the office. "There really is a God!" Many of my colleagues looked up. They had detected my excitement. "Listen to this," I shouted, unable to control myself. "In early September, the Center for Theology and Natural Sciences (CTNS) will be convening a gathering to discuss 'Scientific Perspectives on Natural Evil.'"

"Bingo" shouted someone from behind a desk. I raised my hand in a flat-palmed braking gesture.

"Wait for it," I said. "It gets better. It says here that this is all taking place at the Vatican Observatory." The office descended into total silence. Then a lone voice. It was Charlie again.

"The Vatican has an *observatory*?"

Indeed, it does. The *Specola Vaticana* had several forerunners before Pope Pius XI, in the 1930s, re-sited the modern observatory with the acquisition of two new telescopes in the papal summer palace of Castel Gandolfo in the Alban Hills, some twenty-five kilometers south-east of Rome. In 1993 the observatory was moving into bigger territory, completing the construction of the Vatican Advanced Technology Telescope (VATT) on Mt. Graham, Arizona, probably the best astronomical site in the continental United States. All this from an institution which had imprisoned Galileo and taken until 1992 under Pope John Paul II to issue a formal *mea culpa* for disputing his contention that the Earth really did revolve around the Sun. As the theologian Bernard Lonergan put it so succinctly, "The Church always arrives on the scene a little breathless and a little late."[1]

The Google link showed me a list of all the would-be participants: an impressive litany of theologians, Christians all, but academics with a strong interest in science. Much of this was down to CTNS's founder, a science teacher named Robert John Russell, who had set it up in 1981 with the purpose of strengthening ties and understanding between theology and branches of physics and biology. The first CTNS gathering had convened in 1988 on Vatican soil and this was to be the latest in a series of extended seminars on "God's divine action in the natural world". The tsunami events undoubtedly would be figuring in a major way and here, like manna falling from heaven, was a gilt-edged opportunity to attempt at least some partial resolution of my theodicy quandary. All these experts under one roof and with decades of thinking between them on the fraught question: "Was this really the best that God could have done?"

"What happens if they don't agree to let us in and film," asked one of the team members in the office. "It looks very much like a private event. They may not take too kindly to the presence of cameras there."

1. *Time*, April 20, 1970.

This was a moot point. Even trickier was the fact that this was taking place in the same territory as the Pope's private summer palace at Castel Gandolfo. Acquired by the Holy See in 1596 when the Savelli family were unable to repay its debts to the papacy, the complex, set in one hundred and thirty-five acres of land, boasted a seventeenth-century villa and a farmhouse. During World War Two, church authorities had sheltered thousands of Jewish refugee families here, away from the view of the state authorities, and part of the Pope's palace was converted into a nursery.[2] Moreover, in addition to the observatory, it now laid claim to a swimming pool, installed amidst some controversy by Pope John Paul II, the media-savvy Pole who is now officially recognized as a saint by the Roman Catholic Church.

This was not going to be easy. As it was Vatican territory, if I were to observe the usual permissions protocol, I would have to go through the Holy See's press office. Apart from all the usual bureaucratic delays, there was a further obstacle. Previous full-length documentaries I had made, which had entailed filming in Rome, had included topics such as homosexuality in the Catholic priesthood and the thorny issue of the sexual abuse of minors and cover-ups in the ranks of the hierarchy. Not to put too fine a point on it, even though I was not strictly speaking *persona non grata*, I was probably very close to being somewhere near a very dark shade of gray on a potential blacklist. The fearsome Marjorie Weeke, an American journalist who had zealously marshalled much of the Vatican's relations with the world's broadcasting media for more than thirty years, had retired back in 2001. But many of my contacts had suggested that she had been kept on a retainer as an informal consultant and if my name were to be dangled in front of her, I think we could safely assume an instantaneous veto on our request. We needed another way in.

I thought long and hard about it overnight. The following day, I met the production team for coffee and unveiled my "Plan B".

"The observatory is run by the Jesuits," I told them, having dug around for more information late the previous night on my laptop at home. "It is headed by a Father George Coyne. I'm sure I can explain that it would be better if he just invited us in without going through the usual hoops as it might take too long and a precious opportunity might be missed." Nodding heads all round.

"Maybe you can play the Catholic card?" said Charlie. "I mean, it hasn't done you any harm before."

2. Allen, "Pope's palace."

An hour or two later, I had managed to get Father Coyne to come to the phone. I didn't pull any punches and laid out in great detail what we had filmed so far and that we were looking to Castel Gandolfo for a definitive climax to the documentary.

"Well, I don't know about that," he quipped. "Given the historical rivalry between Jesuits and Dominicans historically, do you think we should be letting an ex-Dominican friar in amongst us?" He continued with a gentle warning. "And don't come here thinking we have all the answers. We don't. And we're a team here at the observatory. I'd need to run it past them and also Bob Russell at Berkeley who heads the conference program." Then he ended with the words that made me want to dance. "But I've a good feeling about this project. I think it'll be fine."

As an experienced film maker of more than twenty-five years I knew that an essential aspect of such initial contacts is to give people the assurance of control. I gave my word that if there were sessions where we were not welcome to take the camera and microphone, then they would have the final word and we would only tread where we were welcome.

"It's going to be nine or ten days," Father Coyne had told me. "You surely wouldn't want to be here for all that time?" There is no way our budget would have stretched to that and, moreover, people sitting around conference tables, no matter how interesting the content editorially, had a limited appeal in terms of televisual images.

"We'd need to film the observatory and explain the work you all do there," I said, partly in honesty and partly as a way of making our visit appear as a way of promoting the work of the Jesuit Order.

"Of course, of course," said Father Coyne. "Give me your number and let me get back to you." In journalistic telephone transactions this can often mean, "I have absolutely no intention of ever communicating with you again," but he seemed genuine enough.

The next day, true to his word, he called back. "In principle, it's a green light," he said. I punched the air with my left fist. "We're going to need all the names of your team. Passport numbers and all the usual security checks."

"Will all this be shared with the Vatican press office?" I asked nervously.

"No, I think we can get all this done without putting them to any trouble," he said. "Pope Benedict was only elected six weeks ago, and they must be so very busy." A *modus vivendi* had been reached. Those good old Jesuits—always top of the league in the *savoir faire* stakes.

In early September 2005 we departed London for Fiumicino airport in Rome where we were greeted by the tiny figure of Stefano Generali and his van. Stefano had to be Italy's shortest and most charming sound recordist. We had worked together twice before and, unusually for an Italian technician, he had excellent English.

"Ciao bello," he shouted as we embraced. "You really pick hard topics for films, don't you? Gay priests, clerical sex abuse and now . . . God and suffering in the world." I shrugged my shoulders. "Why don't you do something nice and easy next time?" It was a question I had asked myself more than once in the last few weeks.

It took us around an hour to make it out to the Alban Hills south-east of the capital. And what a captivating setting. Castel Gandolfo was home to only around ten thousand local inhabitants, but the small town was perched above the majestic Lake Albano below. If you strained your eye, you could make out a chain of holiday villas nestling by the extensive shoreline. Beyond, shimmering in the late summer heat, were the gentle undulating Alban Hills. I could now see why Pope Clement VIII, at the end of the sixteenth century, had parted with one hundred and fifty thousand scudi for this imposing building, set high above one of Italy's most seductive panoramas. The entrance to the Papal Palace was located through an imposing archway situated right in the main town piazza. Swiss guards checked our paperwork and then called up to the observatory offices. Within minutes we were being whisked in and introduced to the director, Father George Coyne. And not a hint of a press officer in sight.

"Come in, come in," he said, heartily.

After a round of introductions, he was ushering us onto a huge terrace which overlooked the magnificent lake below. We had arrived at a good time. The dozen or so members of the symposium were breaking off from their afternoon deliberations and spilling out onto the balcony for refreshments. I mingled among them, making my first acquaintances with people whose names I had known from my extensive reading prior to our departure for Banda Aceh in Sumatra. Never in my wildest dreams had I imagined meeting them in the flesh, nor having them become part of the film. I established that each of them had been charged with the responsibility of preparing a paper for discussion. These had been worked on prior to travel to Rome and circulated widely among the group beforehand. It was a thoroughly impressive and professional operation. In the two or three days we had here, we were going to have to be selective. So I set about finding out what each person's proposed contribution might be and working out how we might set aside time for individual one to one interviews in such a way that did not detract from their main time with the group.

One huge advantage of the location was that there was ample space for us to stay on the premises. So much potential filming time in television is spent getting lost, navigating your way across strangely unfamiliar cities in gridlock (and GPS was still not an everyday feature of rented vehicles in 2005). So, to be two floors up from the main conference gathering, with a view of Lake Albano, and knowing that the newly installed Pope Benedict XVI was only a few hundred meters away in his own secured wing of the summer palace did a lot to put the mind at rest. That night I looked once more through my notes knowing that the real work would start in the morning. In a similar way to how I had felt urged into prayer on the plane descent into London a few weeks previously, I allowed myself some minutes of silence. "Use this time to make your point" I said tentatively to that force, that presence which I hoped was the underpinning focus of everything. What an arbitrary three letter word "God" is. Then as soon as I had finished, I fell asleep.

The following morning after breakfast, we were given a brief tour of the observatory by Father Chris Corbally, and we positioned our camera to take maximum effect as the enclosed shutter panels in the wooden roof slowly pulled back and the solar telescope was moved expertly into position. (This was done purely for our visiting cameras of course. Most astronomy and examination of the heavenly bodies is done after sundown, although I am told the planet Mercury is more easily visible during the daylight hours.) Then we gently stole into the first conference session of the day. In the chair was a rare thing at this gathering, a female of the species! Professor Nancey Murphy taught Christian Philosophy at Fuller Seminary in Pasadena, California and was addressing the delegates with a paper entitled: "Suffering as a by-product of a finely-tuned cosmos". The very first phrase I heard her utter was "crustal recycling". This was a reference to a New York Times article with the intriguing title, "Deadly and Yet Necessary, Earthquakes Renew the Planet".[3]

"If we have a movable crust, we're going to have earthquakes, and if we have earthquakes underwater, we're going to have tsunamis," she said. "But if we didn't have a crust that moved, basically the whole surface would be smooth and, given the amount of water on it, it would be marshland

3. Broad, William, *NYT* Science Section, January 11, 2005.

all over. So you could have basic forms of life, but certainly not complex creatures like us."

Just when you thought tectonic plates were agents of the devil, here was an entirely different take on the *tekton* (Greek for "builder"). It forced land and mountains above water, which ensured we weren't destined to remain largely water-based amphibians. Even more intriguingly, said the New York Times piece, this occasional churning at the earth's surface replenished the upper layers with nutrients. "The volcanoes of the recycling process make rich soil ideal for producing coffee, sugar, rubber, coconuts, palm oil, tobacco, pepper, tea, and cocoa," said its author. "Water streaming through gashes in the seabed concentrates copper, silver, gold, and other metals into rich deposits that are often mined after plate tectonics nudge them onto dry land." Space probes of more than seventy planets and moons in the solar system had suggested that the plate tectonic feature was a quality restricted to planet Earth. Without these thirteen moving, interlocking plates, Homo sapiens would never have had the necessary conditions for the complex twenty-first-century life that we know. So, with crustal recycling, what works amazingly at the systemic level brings with it unavoidable carnage for those poor individuals who are unfortunate enough to be living near its cutting edge.

This picture of ambiguity in nature, with creative and destructive forces being the inseparable two sides of the same coin, I had encountered in my travels out east. But here were some top-class minds taking it to very detailed levels. Thankfully, when their deliberations in Rome were over, all their work was collated into once central volume, a tome that would occupy you for weeks if you were thus inclined.[4]

Nancey had given an excellent example of this value/disvalue dichotomy. There was a lot of talk of entropy and the second law of thermodynamics as a much more convincing explanation for death and disease than blaming Adam and Eve's rebellion. Basically, in any process of change in a thermally isolated system, there needs to be a continual injection of energy, material, or nourishment. Without it, any system tends to run down or to undergo eventual dissolution. That need for new energy has to come from somewhere—which means that the objects in that universe will at each stage have to undergo continuous dismantling and rearrangement. As CTNS's director, Robert John Russell, put it in his submission to the group, "since God's only choice in creating life by natural means is to create through the

4. Murphy et al., *Physics and Cosmology.*

requirements of evolutionary biology, that is variation and natural selection, the consequences of this choice—natural evil—are unavoidable. This means that biological and physical evils will be constitutive of life."[5]

But was this "God's only choice?" This was a matter for further discussion. I do wish that Covid-19 had exploded prior to this gathering, as it would have provided another excellent test case for those gathered. I am sure the response would have been something along the lines of the desirability of genetic mutations being central to our evolving as complex organisms. Basically, mutations are essential for our diversity, and without diversity natural selection could not have contributed to our advancement. Without genetic variation we would all be clones, but it is that self-same variation which makes some of us with certain genes susceptible to cancers and the like. The onward march of the SARS-2-Cov-2 virus throughout the world since January 2020 proceeded through exactly the same process that lies at the heart of the movement and transfer of DNA which forms the evolutionary basis of complex human creatures. And, for some perspective, in any twenty-four-hour clock from Big Bang to the present day, allowing for the fact that some 98 percent of all species that ever lived on planet Earth have now been eliminated, modern day humans would appear on this timescale just a few minutes before midnight. We are the result of an extraordinary chain of biological events. It makes some marvel and wonder. Others take a rather dimmer view: "What a book a devil's chaplain might write on the clumsy, wasteful, blundering, low and horridly cruel works of nature," as Charles Darwin wrote.[6]

I had been very taken with Nancey Murphy's exposition on "crustal recycling" in the context of the devastation brought about by the tsunami. In between sessions, I asked her for a private conversation on camera. We moved away from the conference proceedings and took up a position on the edge of the terrace overlooking the lake below. Nancey was perched somewhat precariously on a low wall as we began our conversation. I cast my mind back to my father's assertion "God could have stopped that", and asked Nancey why a divine creator couldn't intervene, from time to time, to reduce the degree of suffering. In such a world, natural events would obey the laws of nature *most* of the time, but ever so occasionally, couldn't God reserve the right to step in and act as a kind of brake on things?

5. Russell, "Physics, Cosmology," 123.

6. Letter of correspondence to Sir James Hooker, July 10, 1856.

"If the world weren't predictable, then we couldn't be held responsible for our actions," she said. Then she took a sudden, rather startling look down over the wall to the twenty meter drop below. "Suppose it were the case that sometimes when people fell off walls God sent his angels and—and lifted them up, and other times didn't, and you came and—and gave me a push, presuming that God would send his angels; clearly God would send an angel for someone like me, right? But suppose God didn't. Nancey is dead. You—we—just can't act morally in a—in a universe where God might or might not come along and undo the nasty consequences of our nasty actions."

For humans to exercise autonomous moral choices, so goes the argument, they have to act in a world where there is total consistency and predictability in the natural world around them. Science, as we know it, could not operate in a material world in which certain laws were somehow abrogated and put aside from time to time, willy-nilly. In the realm of moral evil also, where human sin is responsible for the suffering of individuals, it is common to find a defense for God that appeals to the need for some operational consistency. If a divine agent intervenes just once to "correct" the unwanted consequences of selfish and evil human choices, then where does it all stop? Does God intervene a bit of the time, some of the time, or all of the time? What then of human freedom and autonomy? "To *ensure* the outcome of free action is a logical contradiction", as the renowned philosopher of religion D.Z. Phillips puts it.[7] Or, in the words of another heavyweight contributor in this field, Alvin Plantinga, "A world containing creatures who are sometimes significantly free (and freely perform more good than evil actions) is more valuable, all else being equal, than a world containing no free creatures at all."[8] All well and good. But it still leaves me asking a fundamental question: in the horrors of the Holocaust, why does God appear to prioritize the freedom of the Nazis to unleash such evil over the need to protect innocent creatures? Put another way, as a Jew in Auschwitz, I would have been absolutely delighted for God to curb some aspects of human freedom if it had improved my chances of survival. A number of Jews found belief in God simply unsustainable amidst the killing machine unleashed by the Third Reich, declaring that if such a God did exist then he had surely broken any sense of covenant with his people. Remarkably, this was not the case for everyone. The late UK Chief Rabbi, Lord Jonathan Sacks, reflecting

7. Phillips, *Problem of Evil*, 98.
8. Plantinga, "Good, Evil," 85.

on the story of Cain and Abel, the first instance of murder in the Bible, puts it this way: "When God speaks and human beings refuse to listen, even God, as it were, is helpless."[9] When asked where God was in the Shoah, he answered quoting the stories of holocaust survivors: "many of them felt that God was with them, giving them the strength and courage to survive. There were people who lost their faith at Auschwitz, there were people who kept their faith, and there were people who found faith at Auschwitz."[10] If you can actually be born *into* religious faith by your experience of the concentration camps, then I suppose all bets are still very much on.

As we approached the end of our first full day of filming at the observatory, my brain was aching somewhat. So much of our shooting of the documentary in the Indian Ocean had been a physical trial: the humidity and extreme heat, the terrible near-impassable roads. We went many days with not an awful amount to eat and drink. But this was a trial of another nature, for here I found myself sandwiched between immensely gifted individuals who had been devoting decades of their professional lives to deliberating on this vexed issue. I did feel like a complete novice as I sat there in those sessions, straining to concentrate and follow the gist of the arguments. Thankfully, there was the oasis of the terrace. In the evenings, the wine flowed copiously. The late setting sun cast marvelous shards of twinkling light on the surface of Lake Albano. And with the group breaking up into smaller numbers I felt able to mingle more easily among them. I lost track of how many times my opening gambits reverted to: "I may have misunderstood your paper entirely, but were you in essence trying to claim that ..." These men and women were gracious and patient to a fault. And perhaps they were, in some small part, glad we were there? I mean, "God and Evil" hasn't exactly been a TV ratings chart topper over the years, has it? We planned, in three months' time, to put that right, of course.

Another gloriously sunny day greeted us over breakfast on the terrace the following morning. I had taken a quick look at the day's agenda and noted that, among the many papers to be discussed, was one which would have the suffering of non-human creatures at the forefront of deliberations. Anthropocentrism remains a constant pitfall in these discussions, and any theodicy worth its salt had to address not only human pain and death, but also Tennyson's description of "nature, red in tooth and claw"[11]. When I

9. Sacks, "God and Holocaust."
10. Sacks, "God and Holocaust."
11. Tennyson, A, *In Memoriam* A.H.H.: Canto 56. 1850.

spent two years with the Dominican order back in the 1980s, I had read far
and wide and had been hugely taken with the writings of my Dutch fellow
friar, Edward Schillebeeckx, who had spoken of a "barbarous excess" of
suffering and evil in our history.[12]

I recalled to mind before the session got under way the example that
wildlife British TV presenter, David Attenborough, had written about
a worm in Africa that can burrow its way into a young child's eye and
cause permanent blindness. Heading the session was a lecturer from the
theology department of my alma mater, Exeter University, Christopher
Southgate. He proposed an examination of "good–harm analyses", a kind
of cost–benefit calculation of positives and negatives in the natural world.
Up for discussion were orcas and the manner in which they preyed on and
killed sealions. Observations had revealed that these killer whales would
frequently toss their victims playfully in the air and prolong their agony.
The speaker said that dolphins had been observed hurling themselves onto
beach rocks in a self-destructive panic in an effort to avoid their predators.

At an individual level, all this looks appalling, but focus on a systemic
level leads one to reflect on certain long term developmental gains. The
more aware, and ably mobile, escape detection. Survival ensures the passing on of genes and an enhancement of the species. Southgate, in his shared
submission to the symposium, quoted a remarkable phrase from the dis-
tinguished philosophy professor, Holmes Ralston III, from his 1987 work
Science and Religion: a Critical Survey: "the cougar's fang has carved the
limbs of the fleet footed deer." Just like the tsunami: tectonic plates that
are good for the whole system combined unavoidably with tragic points of
casualty in specific pressure points.

A silence descended on the group as we neared the end of the morning session. Then, out of the blue, a quite extraordinary acoustic intervention. We were treated to the sound of Schubert being played just down the
corridor. This wasn't an audio recording, but "live". A whispered phrase
punctured the proceedings: "Is it him?" The purported pianist was none
other than the newly elected Pontiff, Pope Benedict XVI. The observatory
territory had been clearly delineated to ensure that the frontiers between
the Jesuit community and the papal summer palace were strictly kept apart.
A Swiss guardsman was positioned half-way down the corridor, this side of
two rather forbidding large wooden doors, to ensure that the Pope's privacy
and territorial integrity were observed at all times. For some two minutes

12. Schillebeeckx, *Christ*, 725.

we listened respectfully to the slow movement from one of the Schubert piano sonatas. Joseph Ratzinger, formerly Archbishop of Munich and then Cardinal at the Holy See's Congregation for the Doctrine of the Faith, was known to come from an exceptionally musical family. His elder brother, Georg, was Herr Domkappellmeister and in charge of the choir at Regensburg Cathedral. We had been discussing, in effect, the mutual inseparability of the beauty and ugliness intrinsic to the created world for the best part of two hours—and we ended it on this.

When this session ended, I was the first out to make a beeline for the coffee trolley outdoors. In all my seven years as an undergraduate, a novice friar, and then postgraduate, I had never had to concentrate as intently. I had a burning question, one that has possibly already formulated itself in your mind too. If God is omnipotent, then why hasn't God in these calculations of value/disvalue, simply caused the natural world to be brought about by divine fiat in a suffering-free manner? Or to put it another way, is this, obeying all those laws of entropy, the evolutionary model and the second law of thermal dynamics, the only show in town?

I tried to collar as many viewpoints on this as possible in between sessions with the various participants. By and large, the consensual view that was scientifically credible was around a position that we might call "the only way". This is a position that Christopher Southgate, in particular, has advanced since the 2005 conference.

> I cannot give a definitive account of why it was metaphysically impossible for an utterly transcendent, utterly sovereign God, the God to whose glory the wondrous scale of the universe bears witness, to give rise to a suffering free world . . . *Scientifically* the notion that this is the only sort of universe where values of beauty, ingenuity, and diversity could *evolve* (as opposed to being beamed down by divine *fiat*) is highly plausible. Up to now . . . I have added to that scientific guess the theological assertion that the God confessed in Christ would not have used a Darwinian process if a less suffering-filled process were available.[13]

In other words, if the observation of complex, freedom-loving creatures made in the image of God, such as ourselves, were to exist on another planet, but in a context where suffering and pain were much reduced due to a markedly different arrangement of the laws of nature, then we would have

---

13. Southgate, "Essays," 915.

a strong case against God. But, at least so far, no such damning comparative alternative has been discovered.

"There's a fairly strong consensus in most scientific circles that the fundamentals of laws of nature would be pretty constant across the universe," one of the symposium delegates told me in a chance exchange over tea in between sessions, "so you won't find many people holding out much hope that there's a death-free, pain-free physical world lurking out there somewhere."

The inferred position of those who cleave to "the only way" position, is that in a material world, you can no more make it devoid of pain and death, than you could make two and two equal five, or produce a string quartet comprised of three instruments only. God cannot make me exist and not exist simultaneously. It is no restriction of God's power to say he cannot do what is logically impossible to do.

When I was a young Dominican friar, I would have long and detailed discussions with my novice master, the renowned student of St Thomas Aquinas, Father Herbert McCabe OP, about such matters. Many years later, a rather splendid collection of my former tutor's words was collated in which he is quoted as saying, "The only reason why you would have to say he [God] can't make square circles is that you can't mention them, the words cancel each other out so that you haven't named anything."[14]

In summary, talk of a pain-free material world would be a classic oxymoron. Over a much-needed glass of chianti, the director of the Vatican Observatory, Father George Coyne, the man who had helped me circumvent the press office to gain access to these rarefied discussions, invoked scripture to make the point.

"Scripture is full of, and Catholic tradition is full of, examples," he declared, filling up my glass. "'Unless the grain of wheat falls into the ground and dies, next year you will not have wheat.'"[15] Citing an example even more recent than the Indian Ocean tsunami, that of Hurricane Katrina in the deep south of the USA, this wise elderly Jesuit was adamant that physical good and physical evil were inseparable. "That hurricane in New Orleans was part of a process of heat exchange—the transfer of energy from one continent to another. Without this process, this planet would be uninhabitable for human beings," he insisted.

These reflections of what is "good" and "destructive" in nature run huge risks of a human-centered myopia. Our criteria rarely revolve around

14. McCabe, *God Matters*, 26.

15. John 12:24.

what is good for the systemic whole, but on the impact on Homo sapiens, now numbering seven billion and eliminating species from habitats at a record background rate. Some years ago, I recall, on a trip to central America, a conversation with a humble agricultural laborer in El Salvador who I met as he was returning from the fields. He had been harvesting *frijoles*, red kidney beans, and had paused on the street to mop his brow and dig deep into his satchel for some much-needed water. I told him that I was not in great shape after contracting a spot of bone-shattering dengue fever on a trip to Guatemala. He sympathized and said I was lucky, as the dreaded chikungunya disease was said to be even more debilitating.

"Mosquitoes," I had shouted in desperation. "What is the point of these creatures, apart from inflicting horrendous diseases on humans? What was God's purpose in the tiny mosquito?" A pause and another wipe of the brow.

"You obviously know little about mosquitoes," I was told. "Of the more than four hundred types of insect, only a handful are harmful to humans," he said with great authority. "They are incredibly effective pollinators. Orchids and other plants rely on such activity. What is more, mosquito larvae are rich sources of food for frogs, lizards, spiders, and a wide variety of fish. So, think about that the next time you hear one of those pesky gnats making that high-pitched noise in your ears at night."

I felt suitably admonished. So, the next time I go down with Zika or the West Nile virus, I will pause and apply some gentle restraint to my anti-mozzie rants.

Since the beginning of the twentieth century, the Newtonian understanding of a predictable clockwork nature to this material world has been firmly put to one side. Einstein's relativity theory, giving way to later discussions on chaos theory, the randomness of activity of sub-atomic particles, dark matter, and so-called "multiverses", are all proof positive that scientific inquiry never stands still. Those of a religious bent talk increasingly of the indeterministic nature of creation and of a vulnerable God "taking a risk". Creation, they say, is not a process which explains what happened 1.4 billion years ago with Big Bang, it is what unfolds unpredictably with every passing moment.

Just when I was attempting to get my head around all this, late into the afternoon came another heavyweight set of deliberations. During these, there was fairly constant reference to the "anthropic principle", and something called "fine-tuning". These ideas have become associated in particular with two cosmologists, John Barrow and Frank Tipler, thanks to their groundbreaking 1985 work, *The Anthropic Cosmological Principle*. Whether it be electromagnetic force or gravitational energy, even the slightest increase or diminution of these fundamentals would make human existence impossible. It has been estimated by physicists that if the strength of gravity were different by just one part in 10^{60}, there could be no stars and galaxies. A tiny bit stronger and all the matter would have collapsed back in on itself; a tiny bit weaker and the matter would have spread out too quickly for anything like galaxies or stars to be able to form. Any serious study of temperature and gas level variations across our galaxy on different planets would lead to the hasty conclusion that the earthly home is a pretty neat fit for Homo sapiens.

By itself, the anthropic principle doesn't clinch any argument about the ultimate origins of the created world. To the scientist of a religious persuasion like Sir John Polkinghorne, it is all too much of a coincidence to be dismissed as anything other than intended by God. Quoted in an article by Edward B. Davis, Polkinghorne states: "It is not a mere happy accident, but it is a sign that the mind of the Creator lies behind the wonderful order that scientists are privileged to explore."[16] Others shrug their shoulders and retort that the evolution of the physical world may well be a one chance in several billion in terms of all the possible variables, but that, in itself, is not proof of an ultimate cosmic designer. It is what it is. Full stop. At this point you pays your money and you makes your choice.

Which leaves me with one almighty question and one which may have occurred to you also as you read this. If you can't create without the mixture of rainbows and tornadoes, life-giving genetic mutation and corrosive cancer, tectonic plates whose seismic shifts make agriculture possible but which kill humans at key pressure points, then why create at all? Is it all worth it? At the micro level it is a calculation that faces any young couple planning a family. Your progeny will inevitably suffer and die in this material world. Faced with an unnerving future in which climate catastrophe and ecological degradation make human life distinctly unstable in the generations to come, some young women have opted to go on "birth strike" and decline the wonders and challenges of parenthood. However, this is still a minority (though growing) outlook on life. And how many of us, given the choice, would press the erase button and cease to have this imperfect material world at all as a price for eliminating life's downsides? Very

16. Davis, "Motivated Belief."

few I suspect. But we are lesser mortals. God is the supreme foundation of the whole project. Was it all justifiable?

During my days as a friar, in addition to reams of theology and scripture, I devoured many of the great European literature classics. One of these, which made an enduring impression, was Dostoevsky's *The Brothers Karamazov*. The key relationship is between Alyosha, a devout seminarian, and the worldly-wise and somewhat cynical Ivan who makes no secret of his dismissive attitude towards his younger brother's faith and vocation to priestly ministry. In a famous exchange which takes places in a small tavern, Ivan is discussing the suffering of young children in the world and poses him this question:

> "Answer me: Imagine that you yourself are building the edifice of human destiny with the object of making people happy in the finale, of giving them peace and rest at last, but for that you must inevitably and unavoidably torture just one tiny creature, that same child who was beating her chest with her little fist, and raise your edifice on the foundation of her unrequited tears—would you agree to be the architect on such conditions? Tell me the truth."
>
> "No, I would not agree," Alyosha said softly.[17]

If the innocent must suffer, as a price for having a material world at all, can this be justified? This was the question I wanted to explore with one of the Vatican conference's key contributors, Philip Clayton, head of Claremont Theology faculty in Los Angeles. Since day one of my arrival at Castel Gandolfo, I had engaged him in a series of easy and stimulating exchanges, and now I wanted to press him more, this time on camera. I posed him the "Karamazov conundrum":

"That's a tremendous question and if I don't stop in silence before your question then I'd say I don't get it. Anyone who sees the depth of the suffering that happens in our world and answers that question simply, of course, of course it was all worth it, doesn't get it," he told me. He looked out briefly at the huge expanse of the sparkling blue lake below and the hills far beyond on the horizon and then gathered his thoughts again.

"I would love to imagine a divine who stood before that button and wept and somehow at the last minute felt it was better to have us than to have only the divine in eternal emptiness. You and I would probably not push the button. As Ivan argued against Alyosha in *The Brothers Karamazov*, we shouldn't push the button. And that God pushed that button and

---

17. Dostoevsky, *Brothers Karamazov*, Ch. 4.

made creation, hints at a mystery that we don't understand. It hints at a resolution that we only hope for: God will only be God if the outcome is something so far better than what we see around us that it would make it all right. But I can only say that as a wish and a hope and not as an item of knowledge."

You won't be surprised to know that this erudite, sincere answer was met with a very long and respectful silence. "Hope . . . and not an item of knowledge." I didn't know at the time, but Philip Clayton's honest riposte was about to allow me to turn a corner. And it happened because of a continued conversation we had once the camera had stopped turning. Winding our way back up the hill, once the recorded interview had ended, I recall asking him about his faith journey. Had he always believed, as a result of being brought up in a Christian family?

"No," he said quite bluntly. "I had reached the stage in life where I had rejected religious belief, but then something happened to make me think again." Writing this book, I had a foggy and distant memory of him telling me he had responded to a call for help from someone. I couldn't remember who, or in what circumstances, so some sixteen years after that meeting outside Rome, I tracked Philip Clayton down and asked him, via a very long Zoom call at 6 am L.A. time, to give me the narrative in full detail. This is the full-length transcript, verbatim, of that quite remarkable life-changing story:

"I was a student at an evangelical seminary named Fuller in the Los Angeles area and had lost my faith by reading philosophical arguments and just seeing no reason to believe in God. I just came to the conclusion that it wasn't going to work. It was finals week. I had returned from hitchhiking around Europe for six months. I had been working as an illegal immigrant in Germany and at some point, I needed to go back to the seminary. A former parishioner in a church where I had been a youth pastor called up, Bobby Newland, and said, 'I am up on Mount Wilson Observatory about five thousand feet above the valley floor of L.A. I've got multiple sclerosis and I'm going to drive this car over the edge and be done with it.' And I said: 'Don't. Please don't' and the conversation continued, and I said, 'I will drive up and talk to you instead of working for exams.' It was late afternoon, getting dark and all I had was a motorcycle, and I remember getting on that bike. It was going to be an hour's drive. I remember heading up the Angeles Crest Highway on my little motorcycle. And in the hour it took to get there I thought: 'why am I doing this? Why am I doing this? There is no reason given my view of the universe for me to do this. It doesn't make sense.'

And then the second realization was that I could not *not* do this. There is nothing in me that would be able to stop me doing this. The third realization was my action which I cannot *not* do doesn't make sense unless there is a God. And then with that level of realization I came to the conclusion that, whatever I say, I just fundamentally believe in God, in some sort of reality-grounded being that I cannot escape. And I think it's better to give up pretending I don't."

Needless to say, the biker sped up in the nick of time and loss of life was averted. This was the nearest I had ever got to a contemporary Road to Damascus conversion story, with Philip Clayton cast reluctantly as a latter-day St Paul. Yet, as gripping as this life-saving story was, I had a nagging doubt. What had this, ultimately, to do with God? I mean, any self-respecting human being in Clayton's situation would have, purely out of empathy, surely responded in the manner he did? Nothing annoys atheists more (and they are right to feel irked) when sanctimonious religious types go on TV and radio and assert that without belief in God, all morality is doomed to collapse. I concede that stripped of the God equation, ethical choices run the risk of being trapped in a dangerous subjectivism. But it is grossly insulting and wrong to claim that humanists, among others, do not have a respectable ethical basis for dealing with other humans, creatures, and the environment. So, I put it to Philip Clayton that, perhaps deep down, he had been driven in his actions solely by compassionate feelings for a fellow human being.

"No Mark. It was not reducible," he told me emphatically. "It would be like, you have lived with this partner for many years and you say, 'I'm finished with her'. You're getting ready to move out and taking a last walk before telling her it's all over. And you realize that despite everything you say, you just love her. You are just bonded to this particular individual and you cannot walk away. And I know men and women who have had that experience which is a realization at a level deeper than emotion, deeper than thoughts, deeper than any argument you can construct. There is just a particular way in this case that you see the universe and you can't see it otherwise. It was an epiphany. 'My Lord and My God.' Just a realization deep down about oneself."

Clayton, in his writings, now frequently refers to God as "UR", meaning "Ultimate Reality", and prefers to talk of "trusting" in UR rather than "having faith". My reaction to his extraordinary story is part marvel, part envy. I have longed for, and still pine for, such an epiphany. It is stubbornly elusive. As is the way in this seemingly eternal journey of restless enquiry, as soon as one revelation or insight acts as consolation, another quandary asserts itself. And this one is fundamental. So here we have a situation in which God (or Ultimate Reality if you prefer) concedes autonomy to the laws of nature as the necessary context for creatures such as ourselves to make moral choices in a scientifically predictable material world. God cannot step in and transform bullets into flowers *some* of the time that they leave pistols when they are fired, and allow the bullets to fire in others, as human beings could not use their God-given freedom on any sound ethical basis in such an inconsistent world. Agents would not know from one moment to the next if their actions would have violent consequences or not. If God suspended the laws of nature on every occasion, then not only would we become de facto puppets of so-called Ultimate Reality, we would have a materially very different world. If value is dependent on disvalue (think of the tectonic plates again with their hugely systemic beneficial effects), then erasing the negative while preserving the positive, according to many scientists, becomes an impossible feat. And God's omnipotence is not compromised if God is restrained from performing the illogical. So then. A huge question now follows. This God who doesn't forcibly change human free will and does not arbitrarily go "zap" and make the laws of nature occasionally act against themselves: what is the point of belief in God? God, to all intents and purposes, appears so remote and so unengaged that, like Ivan in *Karamazov*, we may well still believe but we simply feel compelled to "return him the ticket".

For me, the key term is contingency. First, I do believe that the question "why is there something rather than nothing?" has lost none of its relevance, ever since the days of my keenly disputed conversations with Father McCabe, my novice master. I used to play Devil's Advocate with him:

"It's a nonsense question" I would say. "Maybe, as causality obsessed creatures, we want to look for a first mover, but what if the universe has existed forever in eternity. It wouldn't need a cause. It is just there." He would smile back.

"That is certainly possible, but it still begs the question, why is there something at all rather than nothing? If you tell me it has always been there, just as a brute fact, then that is an unexplained item of faith. You cannot demonstrate it any more than I can prove God exists. And everything you see around you and measure from sense-perception has been brought about and is contingent on another agent. So why would you arbitrarily assert that the whole material universe has just always been here? That, I repeat, is an item of faith."

I never was good at getting the better of my novice master. And I knew that if I made the dumb move of asking what caused God, he would have standard Christian orthodoxy on his side. As that which is timeless, not an object in the universe and transcendent, asking what *causes* God is as sensible as enquiring whether pineapples are generally sadder than bananas. It is a category distinction error. That is what I call "contingency one". It does not prove anything ultimately. But it does set the human mind off on a journey of enquiry and even a great mind such as Stephen Hawking did entertain, from time to time, in all his discussions of black holes and multiverses, that "God" was not a concept that could be ruled out (even if the consensual view is that Hawking died as a non-believer in 2018).

Contingency two is a statement about the human condition. It is best evoked in the famous words from St Augustine in his fifth century classic, the Confessions: "You have made us for yourself, and our hearts find no peace until they rest in you."[18] There is an element to the human spirit that craves communion with the beyond. Call it "the Infinite" or "Eternity", or Philip Clayton's UR, "Ultimate Reality". One of the most religious films I think I have ever seen, and this may come as a surprise to some readers, is Steven Spielberg's 1982 science fiction classic, *ET—Extra Terrestrial*. The constant refrains of "ET phone home", which gather pace and intensity as the movie progresses, depict a stranded alien who is desperate to be re-united with his own kind on his mother planet. If you will pardon the pun, this really is *alienation*. There is a restlessness, an *ennui* if you will, at the root of ET's being that has him pining for communion with his origins. This woundedness at the heart of the human story has occupied boundless authors down the ages. From the psalmist who likened our desire for union with the divine to a "deer that yearns for water", to Plato in his Symposium, through to Simone Weil who gave us a modern version of the Augustinian formula: "At the center of the human heart is the longing for an absolute good," she writes, "a longing which is always there and is never appeased by any object in this world."[19] To counter this, an army of existentialist thinkers would simply retort that there is no necessary correlation between such a desire and a God-centered destination for such longings. If life is ultimately stripped of ultimate meaning and purpose, this human pining

18. Augustine, *Confessions*, Book 1, Part 1, 21.

19. Weil, "A Profession of Faith."

for communion is just one of many of life's absurdities. The joke is on us. We are born. We live. We die and feed the worms. Enjoy music, poetry, and aesthetics if you are lucky enough while your heart beats and your lungs respire, but don't assume there is anything that transcends this earthly life.

I have hovered between these polarities many times. I have sat in churches and found myself mouthing words I find foreign and "other". In such situations, I have heard an inner voice saying "come off it, you don't really assent to all this do you?" Recital of the tenets of the faith during mass at the post-sermon moment of the Creed can certainly be occasions of peak discomfort. But, like a boomerang, I keep coming back. Actually, that isn't quite right. I don't really think that the "I" of that sentence is responsible for what is going on here. One Catholic priest in a recent article summed up what he saw as God's tendency to seek out his creatures, citing these words: "I once saw a ceramic plaque in a retreat house that summed this up: 'That which you seek is causing you to seek.'"[20]

Philip Clayton's earlier analogy with the individual who states he wants to break off a relationship but realizes, in the crucial moment, that he is so grounded in such a liaison that he simply cannot will himself to proceed, I find instructive. Relationships, in order to survive and flourish, need constant renewal and reinvention. The reasons why you fall in love and pledge commitment to a person in those early months are not necessarily the reasons why, fifteen, twenty-five years on, you are still together. Sure, there is the business of a promise made in public and that must not be downplayed. But one's understanding and appreciation of that individual's personhood, their essence if you will, undergoes constant reworking and remaking. Flux and change are inbuilt to this process. If it isn't, stasis and boredom can undermine and corrode. And so it is, may I humbly suggest, with whatever we attribute to that three-letter word "God". I have lost track of how many times the model has been smashed, only for it to be remade—in no large part due to the utterances, and life examples of others. We have had "god of the gaps", filling in the holes that science cannot account for, vengeful Old Testament god (add a long white beard if it helps), hell-bent on punishment and control, supernatural being but misunderstood as another thing or object in the universe that "exists" in the way that the planet Mars and a bar of chocolate are said to exist. The late Catholic theologian, Nicholas Lash, was an astute observer of the limits of discourse in this domain. He

---

20. Martin, "Nine Reasons." 4.

claimed that most of the time we are talking about God we utter nonsense. So what *can* we say?

Students of Ludwig Wittgenstein would urge us to perhaps keep our lips firmly closed, as surely God is the supreme example of that "whereof one cannot speak one must remain silent"[21]. The great twentieth-century philosopher urged us to move from the narrow thinking that language could somehow contain and define intrinsic meaning and extolled the necessity of looking at how words, concepts, are used in social interaction. In one of his last works he writes:

> It is not a matter of the *words* one uses, or of what one is thinking when using them, but rather of the difference they make at various points in life. How do I know that two people mean the same when they say they believe in God? And one can say the same thing about the Trinity. Theology which insists on *certain* words and phrases and bans others makes nothing clearer. (Karl Barth) It, so to speak, fumbles around with words, because it wants to say something and doesn't know how to express it. *Practices* give their words meaning.[22]

The release from having to find water-tight definitions that correspond exactly to words, to orienting oneself to examining the way people behave when they invoke faith offers us some partial relief. But even this landscape is fraught with issues. Communities of religious sisters give up their lives and devote themselves to nursing lepers out of "love for God". ISIS militiamen scream "allahu akbar" (God is Great) before decapitating a western journalist. It seems God-talk manifests the same ambiguities in outcomes that the natural world displays in its rainbows/pestilence, sunsets/tornadoes, and worms: the ones that replenish the soil and the ones that burrow into children's eyes and cause blindness.

Reverting to the revered Wittgenstein for one moment, in addition to practice, in his discussions of religious discourse he was also keen to promote the primacy and importance of metaphor in our attempted discussions of transcendence. This opens the way to the language of scripture and revelation as a complement to more abstract discussions of the divine. In our efforts to reconcile the suffering of the world with a benevolent Ultimate Reality, there is the danger that talk of "the first mover", "the ground of all being", and "the uncaused cause of everything" serves the purposes of

---

21. Wittgenstein, *Tractatus*, Part 7.
22. Wittgenstein, *Remarks*, 318.

elite university metaphysics lecturers and their students and perhaps very few others. It is a point acknowledged by Christopher Southgate, one of the Vatican Observatory attendees: "The difficulty with a theodicy that simply asserts that this is the best sort of system God could have created is that such theodicy describes a God who is the creator of systems but not a God who is in loving relationship with creatures. It is my view, therefore, that the best contemporary cosmic theodicies must start from a version of the only-way argument, but they must go on to make other moves that are more focused on God's relationship with the individual creature."[23]

For the dozen men and women gathered at the Vatican Observatory and for millions of other Christians around the world, the God of cosmology who is the "uncaused cause" is also "person". Even if a mother forgets her child, "I will never forget you," says Yahweh.[24] This is the God who knows the numbers of hairs on every head before we were fashioned in our mothers' wombs, the God who lures us into relationships by that sense of incompleteness and contingency mentioned above. And above all, lest this God appear remote, unseen, unknown, for those like me, brought up in Manchester in northern England in the 1960s by my Catholic parents, we were invited to believe that any chasm and rift between the Godhead and humanity is answered by the "logos", the Word, in St John's Gospel. Jesus. "Anyone who has seen me has also seen the Father."[25]

What does God look like? The hiddenness of God, so often invoked by the psalmist, is unmasked by the life of his Son. This is what I am asked to believe. A walking, talking, fully human, fully divine individual is the one born as a fragile child, who heals, sides with the outcasts, has no time for religious "systems" and shallow legalistic pieties, and whose mission ends in a life cut short, abandoned by friends and followers. It has taken me the experience of that tsunami journey and consequent reflection to appreciate the extraordinary parallels between our own siren cries of exasperation at the apparent non-intervention of God in the face of suffering and the fate of Jesus in his passion. "He trusts in God," cry the onlookers at Calvary in St Matthew's Gospel. "Let God rescue him now if he wants him, for he said, 'I am the Son of God'. In the same way the rebels who were crucified with him also heaped insults on him."[26] As Mary, his mother, and the beloved disciple

23. Southgate, "Cosmic Evolution", 158.

24. Isa 49:15.

25. John 14:9.

26. Matt 27:43–44.

John look on at the foot of the cross, were they utterly resigned to the horror unfolding in front of them? Or did Mary, inwardly, join the thousands
of helpless parents down the centuries who have witnessed their children's
lives draining away? Did she feel tempted to look up to the heavens and ask:
"Where are you?" And finally, from the mouth of Jesus himself, "My God,
my God, why have you abandoned me?" This useless God who does not step
in to curb the moral depravities of humans, nor suspend the laws of nature
to rapture up his Son from the clutches of men driven by political agendas.

After we returned from the heady discussions at the Vatican Observatory, we had one final piece of filming to do. This figure of a helpless Jesus
on the cross was the overwhelming image that dominated my thinking. I
pondered the options for where best to film this final minute of our one-
hundred-minute-long documentary and my mind turned to a London
location where I had attended the eucharistic celebration on many an occasion: Westminster Cathedral. On my first visit to London on a school trip in
the late 1960s I had come across the red brick neo-Byzantine structure just
off Victoria Street with its impressive campanile and had mistaken it for a
mosque. (I was not the first nor the last in this regard, of that I am sure.)
Our teacher had explained to us that it was the largest Roman Catholic
place of worship in the United Kingdom and, at more than five thousand
square meters, among the denomination's fifty biggest places of worship in
the world. The huge thirty feet rood or crucifix suspended above the altar
was by far the most impactful aspect of this space for me as a young boy. It
was back to that image I now returned.

The cathedral was based on a marshland area originally owned by
Benedictine monks known as *Bulinga Fen*. In the nineteenth century the
site had been home to a large prison complex. It was only after its destruction that the Roman Catholic Church acquired the land in 1884. No time
was wasted by the architect, John Francis Bentley, and construction was
completed in 1903. The imposing cross, which soars above the altar into the
darkness above had been fashioned in Bruges and transported across the
English Channel. On the final day of our filming, after the 5.30 pm evening
mass, the cathedral authorities closed the doors to the public, and allowed
us a couple of hours to complete the concluding words of my tsunami
journey. Bruno placed his camera in the central aisle and framed me with
the majestic structure looming high above me. And these were my parting
words to the television audience:

"This cross could be the biggest lie ever bestowed on humanity. But equally it could be that God became human precisely to tackle this question of evil and death. And if suffering is the biggest obstacle to faith, what an image to leave with your doubting creatures. A powerless God who says that no account of creation is complete without a final act of redemption. Can I, can you, begin to accept that that is not a hoax, that in the end all may be well? For the first time in my life, I begin to understand a prayer I was taught as a child. Lord, I believe, help my unbelief."

Our final documentary, *Tsunami: Where Was God?* aired in December 2005. As has been previously mentioned, Channel Four, in their wisdom, opted to place it in the schedules on Christmas evening at 8 pm. Merry Christmas and Feliz Navidad a todos! Needless to say, the viewing ratings were understandably pitiful. A mere five hundred thousand switched on. That was around a paltry 2 percent of the total audience. Yet in spite of this, as the weeks and months afterwards revealed, it totally struck home amongst those who were brave enough to resist the Yuletide TV tinsel and make the difficult choice. The film won an inaugural Radio Times viewers' award for the best religious documentary, and a merit award at Lambeth Palace as the Archbishop of Canterbury housed the prestigious annual Sandford St Martin TV and radio awards for religious broadcasting. I joked among colleagues that this had been the only film I had ever made that had gained more awards than it had viewers.

And that, I guess, should have been that. Except it wasn't. You can't put an enormous dilemma like this to bed once and for all. In spite of what I had said with that huge crucifix suspended above me in Westminster Cathedral, I can't claim to have "answered" the conundrum or solved the riddle. And that, as I came to discover in the ensuing years as I put the film well and truly behind me and endured more and more restlessness, was precisely the problem. In construing all this principally as a "riddle", I was selling my own humanity and faith tradition short.

In some form or other, I needed to move on—from *explanation* to *encounter*.

6

"Unless I See the Scars of the Nails . . ."

IT WAS THE DECADE in which the young Elvis exploded onto the music scene and the USA and the Soviet Union were going head-to-head in the so-called "space race". I had just made it into the 1950s by a whisker, born in our terraced house at 70 Manchester Road at 3.30 pm on the winter solstice—December 21,1959. In the northern hemisphere this is the shortest, darkest day of the year. In a cash-strapped family such as ours, its proximity to Christmas came with the entirely understandable opportunities for belt-tightening. "This is one present for birthday and Christmas. You'll understand—we're a bit short this year," was a not untypical Advent refrain. Financial pragmatism began early. I would ask for cash for my birthday and use the funds in the next couple of days to buy my relatives their presents for the big day four days later. Where it was possible, I would talk up the idea with my two brothers that the more money they gave me, the better chance they had of getting something half-decent when Santa popped down the chimney.

If a birthday on the twenty-first had its drawbacks, it also came with a plus. It was the feast of St Thomas the Apostle, a biblical figure who I came to identify with more and more as questions emerged in adolescence and beyond about the fundamentals of my Catholic faith. For this was "Doubting Thomas", surely the hero of any post-Enlightenment faith, where so much is staked on verifiability, observation and personal experience. I always felt sorry for Thomas. In John 11, Jesus hears the news that his dear friend Lazarus is gravely sick and proposes to return to Bethany to attend to him. This is a dangerous move as Jesus has just been the target of a stoning attack by religious leaders. This part of Judea was hostile territory. Yet it does not stop Thomas declaring: "Let us go there also that we may die with him."[1] After Jesus's death and reported sightings, you can imagine Thomas's possible feelings of exclusion as a number of the disciples attest to Jesus's appearances and yet he seems to have been frozen out of the action. His outlook on the world, in just a few days, has swung from uninhibited bravery to outright incredulity. "Unless I see the nail marks in his hands and put my finger where the nails were, and put my hand into his side, I will not believe," he declares, defiantly.[2] By these words Thomas locates in Jesus the legacy of his suffering as the *essence of his identity*. Maybe if you or I had lost a close friend in death and they had been reported alive several days later we might be convinced of their enduring existence by their unique way of smiling, a characteristic eccentric way of walking, or something that gives them away, such as a manner of speaking. But for Thomas he can look no further than wounds for "proof". There is no further detail in John's Gospel of the interaction between Thomas and the remaining disciples, but his refusal to accept their word is almost certainly likely to have been a cause of considerable tension. First of all, Thomas is possibly privately irked that he has been excluded (how universal is that human reaction of recoil when one assumes one has been with one's peers on the inside track, only to realize that one is an excluded outlier). Secondly, Thomas's demands effectively cast aspersions on the disciples' veracity. He is, in effect, implying that they are either being taken in by their overactive imaginations or they are pulling a fast one. Eight days pass. Eight days in which Thomas is left to stew on his bitter feelings of exclusion. He is not a part of the in-crowd.

This Thomas story is all so familiar to us that we are perhaps guilty of letting it slip by without noticing some of its rather extraordinary aspects. First of all, his insistence on body-to-body contact, inserting his own fingers into the wounds of Jesus ("Put my hand into his side."). This demand straddles the ground somewhere between revulsion and extraordinary intimacy. In the account of Jesus's appearance to him, he is perfectly prepared to grant the doubter his wishes. "Put your finger here; see my hands. Reach out your hand and put it into my side,"[3] he says. Thomas stops short.

1. John 16:11.
2. John 20:25.
3. John 20:27.

What he has in front of him is more than enough. "My Lord and my God," he exclaims. These, for me as a youngster, are the words we were always encouraged to whisper in the Eucharist at the elevation of the Blessed Sacrament in the sacrifice of the mass. And there is more, much more to say about a story that takes up barely three or four verses in the latter part of John's Gospel.

First, how distinctly strange that this new life of resurrection displayed by Jesus bears all the hallmarks of his earthly suffering. In funeral services, the bereaved are comforted with the notion that in the life beyond, "all tears will be wiped away" and there will be an end to pain and death. Yet John, in his account, presents not some glorified whiter than white account of Jesus's appearance in which all evidence of pain and suffering have been emasculated. On the contrary, these bloody wounds are the very hallmark of Jesus's identity for the doubting Thomas and the gateway to the renewal of his encounter with his risen Lord. And that this should be the evangelist John's account. John, whose language for Jesus is often so abstract, ethereal even: "I am the vine"; "I am the Way the Truth and the Life."[4] From the evangelist's heady exposition of the incarnation of the Word in the prologue of his Gospel to the depictions of bloody wounds in his hands and his side in the new life of resurrection.

After his eight-day wait, Thomas does not encounter Jesus as a private experience. The other disciples are alongside him. This is key, as it reduces any post-hoc possibility for Thomas that he may have been subjected to some solipsistic self-induced hallucination. "Been on the wine a bit too much have we, Thomas?" One can imagine all the rest of the potential skeptical voices that may well have greeted him. This faith is a shared social encounter. Options for deniability are radically reduced when others around you attest to the same experience. And what was the nature of this appearance? A revivified corpse? In 1984, the former Bishop of Durham, the Rt Rev David Jenkins, took the world by surprise when airing his thoughts on Resurrection with BBC radio:

> A conjuring trick with bones only proves that somebody is clever at a conjuring trick with bones. I am bothered about what I call 'God and conjuring tricks'. I am not clear that God maneuvers physical things. I am clear that he works miracles through personal responses and faith ...[5]

4. John 14:6.
5. *Poles Apart.* BBC Radio 4, Oct 4, 1984.

I will confess that I am rather less interested in debates about the literal physical nature of Jesus's new life, than about the question marks surrounding his recognizability. I think I would instantly be able to identify a revivified corpse, especially if it were the representation of a loved one, a family member, or in this case, a cherished and inspiring leader who had been most savagely put to death only a few days beforehand. "Woman why are you crying?" an unrecognized stranger asks Mary Magdalene as she weeps next to the tomb where Jesus has been laid. "Who is it you are looking for?" When she mistakes him for the gardener and demands to know where the body of Jesus has been placed, a one-word answer is enough to move the heartbroken disciple from despair to elation. It is her name. "Mary." It is an Isaiah moment. "Do not be afraid. I have called you by your name. You are mine."[6]

A parallel dynamic is at work in St Luke's Gospel on the road to Emmaus. Here we have two disciples recounting to a complete stranger the events of the Passion and Crucifixion. The evangelist informs us that this man who appears from nowhere is none other than Jesus, but that "they were kept from recognizing him".[7] What elliptical words. I am not persuaded that this was because Jesus was heavily disguised with a coterie of wig, false beard, and a face covering. Mary, after all, moved from ignorance to full acknowledgment at the side of the tomb by a process of sudden interior transformation when she heard her name. This has nothing to do with his external appearance. And it is the same when the Emmaus pair, Cleopas and his companion, invite Jesus to join them to share food. Jesus breaks the bread—an odd detail as he is the guest in the house, but we find him assuming control of the dining rituals. And in that instant, "their eyes were opened". The risen Jesus is known for who he is by his action of *naming* with Mary, by his *breaking of bread* on the road to Emmaus and, with Thomas, because he bears the wounds of his suffering.

In all three scenes, Jesus meets the individuals head on. His act of the naming, that most intimate of gestures. Secondly, by coming into the home of Cleopas and his friend. And, most importantly for the purposes of this work, by meeting Thomas *precisely in his fog of doubt*. I have mentioned my very soft spot for Thomas and the pride I had growing up, knowing that my birthday fell on his feast day. It wasn't to last. Having been inserted into the Roman calendar in the ninth century on December 21, centuries later,

6. Isa 43:1.
7. Luke 24:16.

in 1969, it was thought to be interfering with the pre-Christmas season of Advent. Thomas was in danger of becoming a distraction. So off he went, to July 3. And there he has remained ever since.

What has all this to do with the theodicy quest to reconcile belief in God and the presence of a physical world that, for all its beauty and glory, rains down occasional pain and devastation on humans and is character-ized by the certainty of death? I contend, in the story of Thomas, that there is a deep correlation between profound doubt on the one hand and the evi-dence of Jesus's suffering. If we hark back to the previous chapter and those heady, involved deliberations at the Vatican Observatory, much hinged on our understanding of this physical home we call Earth. We saw a hy-pothesis advanced that testified to the inseparability of value and disvalue in creation and what Christopher Southgate referred to as an "only-way" theory of the natural world. This became an investigation into the very na-ture of matter itself, entropy, generation, and destruction, "unless a grain of seed die and fall into the ground," etc, etc. The Christian claim is that the divine and the material coincide utterly in the figure of Jesus. The two natures coincide completely, in one "hypostasis" or substance, according to the 451 CE Church Council of Chalcedon. This definitive declaration of the church fathers essentially spells out in greater doctrinal detail what is im-plicit in the very opening words of St John's Gospel written more than three hundred years earlier: "In the beginning was the Word, and the Word was with God and the Word was God." That the Word becomes flesh involves an emptying out, or a *kenosis*, to use St Paul's New Testament term, into mat-ter which also carries with it a journey into the inescapable suffering and death, which is the lot of humanity. If Jesus had lived until the age of eighty and died in his sleep after a lifetime of gentle teaching, the claims of those through the centuries that Christ's death and transformation "answer", at least to a degree, the raging questions about God and suffering would have been somewhat weakened. In fact, if my own personal faith obstacle were to assume primacy in demanding a response in the life and death of Jesus (namely the negative side effects inherent in a natural world which ad-vances through evolution), strictly speaking one might have expected the incarnate Word of God not to go to his fate at the hands of murderous men, hell-bent on seeking out a scapegoat for political ends. No, Jesus should have died in an earthquake, a tornado, or by some freak virus that erupted in Judea in the early decades of the first century CE.

It is perhaps an understatement of the highest order to suggest that such a demise may not have met the narrative requirements of salvation history. That is a long and complicated back story and beyond the scope of what we are dealing with here. That this most innocent of innocents had his life vanquished on Calvary as a result of human plotting, betrayal and cowardice is, if anything, a riposte to those whose principal problem with God is the existence of *moral* evil: the perversion of human free will.

And how he suffered. In 2004, along with millions of others, I took myself along to see Mel Gibson's *The Passion of the Christ*. Hollywood was nervous of financing it. Gibson stumped up his own money and the film went ahead. It was translated from a script, originally in English, into Latin and Aramaic. There were accusations of anti-Semitism amidst other controversies. Jim Caviezel, the actor who played Jesus, and assistant director, Jan Michelini, were struck more than once by lightning during the film shoot.[8] The bible epic eventually went on to pull in more than six hundred million dollars at the box office.[9] I admired the spirit behind Gibson's endeavors. However, its depiction of the last twelve hours of Jesus's life did rather suggest that the glory of God's redeeming gift to humanity was directly proportionate to the number of liters of blood on the screen. I have visited far too many Spanish and Latin American churches in my time to witness how blood, anguish and pain almost become an end in themselves in the depictions of the Crucifixion. Do not misunderstand me. I do not wish to airbrush away agony and excruciating pain. Anyone who has paid careful attention to the manner in which victims of the Romans' death sentence specialty would often take several days in which to suffocate slowly as the lungs collapsed under the distribution of weight of the human frame, knows that this activity is humanity at its cruelest. As creatures of empathy, our reaction when faced with the physical suffering of any sentient creature, animal or human, is to flinch, to turn away. Our empathy is part compassion, part self-protection spurred on by projection: *In another scheme of things, that could be me.* When faced with twenty-five minutes of scourging in *The Passion of the Christ*, minutes in which huge chunks of flesh are removed from the human corpus to such an extent that the original bodily form, by the end, borders on the unrecognizable, one is left asking "is this a realistic portrayal or a descent into pornographic violence, because violence sells cinema tickets?"

8. http://news.bbc.co.uk/1/hi/entertainment/3209223.stm.
9. https://www.the-numbers.com/movie/Passion-of-the-Christ-The#tab=summary.

When all is said and done, these are matters of degree. According to the gospel accounts, Jesus is only on the cross a matter of hours, and not days as many of the Romans' convicted criminals were. Not only pain, but humiliation was the intention of the occupying power in its chosen method of execution. The tastefully arranged loin cloths that feature so prominently in hundreds of artistic depictions of Calvary are there to protect our prudish sensibilities. In all likelihood, Jesus was unclothed, defenseless and exposed. To his final breath. "Into your hands I commend my spirit." There are no miraculous interventions. The laws of physics are not put on hold or reversed. No army of angels in a last-ditch rescue act. Just Mary, his mother, John the beloved disciple and a few onlookers, a number of whom cannot resist the temptation to taunt and scorn even at this late, late hour. Where has everyone gone? For three years they followed him and pledged fidelity and allegiance. If you want to ponder the depths of what a pure void, utter meaninglessness, might feel like to a human being, then just make that fleeting journey into that space . . . and recoil. That is what hopelessness looks like. That is what failure feels like. "My God, my God, why have you abandoned me?" And this image is Christianity's calling card to a world hungry for coherence, purpose, and redemption. What a strange business. Jesus: the intersection of time and eternity, of human and divine, "the image of the invisible God, the first-born over all creation".[10] He dies. An uncanny darkness descends. Strange events are reported nearby with earthly tremors and damage to the veil of the holy temple. His limp, lifeless body is taken down from the cross. They depart the scene.

If the story ended there, of course, we'd be saying the very words I uttered when I went in 1973 to see my first performance of *Jesus Christ Superstar* in Manchester's Palace Theatre: "What happened to the Resurrection?" Someone explained to me that the musical was essentially the world seen through Judas's eyes, so that was why it ended on the Crucifixion. It wasn't meant to be a faith snub by the writers and composers. When I retorted that Judas wasn't there on the hill called Golgotha and had probably already by this point taken his own life, I just got a blank stare. I still haven't had an answer all these years on.

When I shared with a friend my intention to meditate on Thomas and his refusal to accept the disciples' testimony, I was asked a direct question by a skeptical companion.

"Do you believe Jesus was actually in that room with Thomas?"

10. Col 1:15.

I retorted with the only words I could find at the time.

"What do you mean by *actually in that room*?" More clarification of the original question.

"What I mean is, if we had set up a video camera and tripod and set the thing running in record before they had all entered that room, would it have registered the presence of Jesus on the playback?" In the twenty-first century, it would appear that belief in the conquering of death by the risen Jesus is all down to CCTV footage.

I thought long and hard about my answer and replied with an analogous example from a contemporary film favorite, the 2009 movie, *Looking For Eric*, directed by the multi-award-winning Ken Loach. It will come as no surprise to those who know me that this figures highly in my rankings because it features a life-long obsession with Manchester United soccer club. Eric Bishop, a salt of the earth postman and lifelong fan, is on the verge of a nervous breakdown. He is estranged from his wife Lily who he has walked out on after the birth of their daughter. Work in the sorting office is proceeding very badly and his stepson is involved with local criminal gangs and shielding a revolver under the floorboards of his bedroom. Postman Eric is riddled with suicidal thoughts and gazes wistfully at a huge poster of his soccer hero, Frenchman, Eric Cantona, on his bedroom wall. This "god" of the game had it all: arrogance, skill, popularity, and devotion from the masses. What a contrast with his own pathetic failure of a life. Out of nothing, he hears a voice with a heavy French accent. He looks over to the other side of the room and there is "King Eric". The postman rubs his eyes. They converse. Over the course of the next few days, the "king" turns mentor and life-coach to the beleaguered postman. There is one especially riveting sequence when they are out jogging together, track suit bottoms and all, and they pass a group of postal workers. The two joggers are running and exchanging animated opinions. Hands are being waved around passionately. Mentor Eric is forcing his tutee to face up to some hard truths, to dig deep and retrieve his youthful elan. However, the onlookers are perplexed. They can only perceive, with their eyes, their colleague from the post office. "Who's he talking to?" one of them asks. Their doubtful looks betray one clear point of view that unites them all: Eric (Bishop) has lost the plot. Now he's even talking to himself. He's on the fast track to the lunatic asylum.

Consider our vantage point as the privileged cinema-based spectator. We see both Erics: celebrity soccer icon and humble postie. We are party to their heated and full-on exchanges. Is what is taking place between these two characters "real" or not? You could argue the toss on both scores, using rather different criteria. What is undeniable is that it is transformational. Over the following days, the man who was on the verge of suicide makes a bold and successful attempt to win back his wife Lily. He lays down the law at home in a manner that shocks his stepson and finds a way to combat the local mafia criminals and extricate his family from their web of menace. When I recounted this analogy to my friend, he was silent for some time.

"Only *you* could juxtapose the Christian Resurrection and the fortunes of Manchester United soccer club," he quipped. Then I reminded him I had once made a TV documentary about whether soccer had become, in effect, the twenty-first-century religion. We had christened the film *Hallowed Be Thy Game*, and in the closing minutes I had outrageously claimed that if there was any such state called "the kingdom of God" it must resemble those few hours after an amazing soccer match. A world in which there are no strangers, a world united by the wonder of everything they have just witnessed, a world in which petty divisions and tribal passions are set aside because of what has been witnessed; the transcendental power of the beautiful game.

Call it coincidence of timing or providence, but I write these words on Holy Saturday, that bleakest, flattest of days in the Christian calendar. Good Friday has ended in a chilled silence. Yesterday we all walked home alone. All we did was ponder and wait. I know within several hours from now there will be bellringing, candles will be lit, and the Easter Paschal Candle will defiantly declare victory over the bondage of death. I have never had a "Thomas experience". I pine for, but cannot say I have ever undergone, that unambiguous epiphany so movingly related by Philip Clayton in the previous chapter. I know I alluded to Resurrection at the end of *Tsunami: Where Was God?* as I walked close to the image of the Crucified One in Westminster Cathedral. "A powerless God who says that no account of creation is complete without a final act of redemption," I had said straight to the camera as the documentary neared its end. Just because you want to believe something does not make it true. We're back to the Gospels. "But what about you?" says Jesus to Peter. "Who do you say I am?"[11] It's a two-thousand-year-old on the spot question that never goes away.

For those with a more robust faith than I possess when they are confronted with the God and Evil dilemma, it normally takes little time before

11. Matt 16:15.

they place what they see as their trump card: the Eschaton. This Greek word, which only appeared in the English language for the first time in 1844, refers to the end times, the second coming of Christ, the end of history as we currently conceive it. The resurrection of Jesus points to a transformation in which, in the fullness of time, God will conform all things to himself. These niggling and persistent questions about the compatibility of God's goodness and the suffering of creatures will be banished. Now this is orthodoxy. One cannot give a full account of Christian hope without some eschatological dimension, and it would be to utterly sell it short if we did. But I am saddled with two questions that continue to dog me. First, why didn't God move straight to such a state in the first place and spare us all the pain and drama of a material world in which glory and tragedy seem inseparable? Was this not possible, desirable? I have yet to hear an account that satisfactorily explains why not. And secondly, perhaps less of a question and more of an observation: do not these fervent believers see the inherent risk of alienating those of hesitant faith by an over-enthusiastic invoking of the Eschaton card? It's a post-apocalyptic version of jam tomorrow. Maybe I've suffered too many incessantly long uncomfortable journeys as a child in the rear of a crowded car in damp clothes, bent double with tummy ache and staring out the window at leaden skies through the northern English drizzle, but there were just too many times when adult consolations of "it'll be all right when we get home" didn't really cut the mustard. Maybe that's because when we got home the heating had broken down and there was nothing in the fridge or larder to provide sustenance. Besides, cleaving to the Eschaton option requires a minimal degree of faith conviction in the first place. And if it's lacking?

But this is not quite a dead end. Or at least, that is how it seems to me. I cannot claim any self-extraordinary "My Lord and My God" experience akin to that of St Thomas. What wavering faith and hope I do profess resides in no small part in the accounts of transformation attested to by those early church followers of Jesus. Saul turns from sadistic persecutor to Paul the tireless scribe, and declares that if Jesus is not risen then our lives are truly in vain. Peter undergoes a metamorphosis from being a cowardly self-preserving denier of Jesus to an indefatigable and fearless preacher. He dies sometime between 64 and 68 CE in Rome under the Emperor Nero, who is seeking scapegoats for the great fire in the city which has wreaked havoc and destruction. Nero finds in Peter and his associates a useful outlet. Peter begs to be crucified upside down because he is not worthy to be killed in the same manner as his Lord. The Apostles in that upper room, cowering and frightened, have previously undergone nothing less than a complete *volte face* in their attitude to risk and danger. Soon they are charging all over Asia Minor and beyond with an urgent zeal to bear witness to the Resurrected Christ. The fearful have morphed into the fearless. How? Why? Is this, cynically, a case of those writing up the history, casting themselves in the most positive light possible? Two thousand years have passed. Centuries of opportunities for scrutiny of sources and texts and motivations. I'm a cynical old hack. Journalists grow up and cut their teeth looking for the basest motives as explanation. Yet despite all my efforts to find fault with the account of transformation, to find cracks and faultlines in the quite remarkable energy and conviction at the heart of the early church, I cannot fail to concede that "something happened". Resurrection is not resuscitation. Nor is it a happy ending tacked on to the tragedy of Good Friday. It is a wiping clean of the slate. It is a whole new beginning.

I alluded in the closing part of the previous chapter to the need to move from *explanation* to *encounter*. Given the fact that physical extinction for me remains, in Shakespeare's words, "the undiscovered country from whose bourne no traveler returns",[12] I'm left looking elsewhere for pointers, signs that suffering in God's less than perfect world might be redeemed. Remember that exchange with Richard Dawkins before we set off on our tsunami mission? He had asked me what plausible reasons I had for believing in God. His unexpected question had caught me off guard. However, in addition to suggesting that the question "why is there something at all rather than nothing" was not without merit as a starting point for enquiry, I had also added, "I'd say I have met, in my lifetime, a very small number of people who exude what I would call 'a peace that surpasseth all understanding'. They have a sense of great calm and holiness about them and that always seems to be rooted in a profound sense of the sacred." What passed between us after those words was just a respectful silence. They were practically my parting words as I bade him farewell on the steps of his imposing house in North Oxford before departing for Indonesia, India and Thailand.

These words came several years before a sighting of another one of these exceptional individuals. On my tsunami journey, I had already nearly been reduced to tears by the sight of Father Xavier, in that church in Velankanni, tending to the poor and hungry as they filed patiently in columns outside his quarters on the upper cloister of his Basilica. He wasn't

12. *Hamlet* Act III Scene 1.

to be the last such person whose life made such a dramatic impact. There was more in store.

In 2013, after the shock resignation of Pope Benedict XVI, the Roman Church broke with precedent; it chose its first Jesuit Pontiff, Jorge Mario Bergoglio, to lead the world's 1.2 billion Catholics. It was the first time the Cardinal electors in their conclave had opted for a man from South America. Little was known about him. There was an information vacuum, as news gathering operations all over the world had prepared biographies on four or five of the most fancied candidates, but Bergoglio had not figured on the list. The Cardinal of Buenos Aires had been a fifty to one outsider. A call from BBC Radio 4: "Mark; what are you up to at the moment. Could you go to Argentina? We need a profile of the new pope: like *now*."

After a fourteen-hour flight, we hit the ground running. Our small team interviewed supporters and critics alike, Pope Francis's sister, and talked to some of his old Jesuit brethren. Then, late into our assignment, we had to go to a place called *Bajo Flores*. This was a very run-down shanty town on the outskirts of the capital and had been a favorite destination of the new pope when he had been Archbishop of the city. From time to time. he would pop down on local transport, disguised in mufti, and mingle with the people. The princes of the Church have developed a reputation over the centuries for being aloof, but here was a pastor who, to quote his own words, was like "a shepherd living with the smell of his sheep".[13] Unemployment in this sector of the city was rife. Decent housing was scarce. Its citizens were the forgotten of Buenos Aires. But not forgotten by a handful of dedicated young clergy, many of whom had constituted a successive missionary presence in the bowels of this neglected enclave. We dedicated one afternoon to a visit and, as I have described elsewhere, the forty-minute journey from our downtown hotel to Bajo Flores came to a climax in a most unusual and unexpected manner.

> Accompanying us was the softly spoken yet gently charismatic Father Gustavo Carrara, a worker priest in his early forties. Everywhere we walked people's faces would light up when they saw him. Elderly women went out of their way to cross the road just to shake his hand. Young kids buzzed around him like bees around early spring lavender. What I was seeing was, in effect, a carbon copy of how Bergoglio had been received on his visits as Archbishop and later as Cardinal. We spent a whole afternoon in Bajo Flores

13. Pope Francis's address to the world's priests at the Chrism Mass on Holy Thursday March 28, 2013.

and when we had finished my producer, Charlotte Pritchard, and I bade farewell to Fr Carrara and the community leaders and climbed into our car, ready for the return to the heart of Buenos Aires. As I looked out of the window, I caught a final glimpse of the inspirational priest and then, in a moment so redolent of that trip on the back of the truck in Banda Aceh (on our tsunami journey), I had non-stop tears flowing down my cheeks. I could see the car driver eyeing me in his mirror. "What is it?" asked Charlotte. "Has someone upset you?" I shook my head vigorously and pointed to the priest who had now turned his back on us in order to return to the heart of the shanty town. "No," I said, through gentle sobs. "It's just that . . ." and I now pointed to him as he grew smaller in the distance. "I could have done that. I *should* have done that."[14]

It is eight years since that happened, but it seems like yesterday. St Paul, in his first letter to the Corinthians, tells us that we are Christ's body and that if one part suffers, every part suffers with it. Thomas saw the wounds on Christ's body and his doubts were cast aside. In the scrapheap of the unwanted not too far from some of Buenos Aires' most fashionable neighborhoods, here was another man who sought to touch the wounds of Christ's body. But unlike Thomas he was not spurred on to do so through skepticism or lack of conviction. To this day I can still draw his face in my mind, hear his reassuring voice, and see his outstretched arms as he walks and comforts those alongside him. Such rare moments as these are the times in my life when I have felt my humanity most engaged, when both intellect and emotion are fused and firing on all cylinders. Such lives have a cursed beauty about them that both invite and accuse. They exert a magnetic pull and yet induce fear: "What would become of me if I followed that example?"

If the dramatic events of two thousand years ago in the life of the early church appear remote, there is a line through saintly women and men down the centuries that keeps the fire burning. When we fixate on the ills and evils of the world with the daily bombardment of murders, rapes, and cruelties that threatens to totally distort our view of the world, we forget that every day, un-newsworthy as it may be, there are hundreds of thousands of people mopping brows, tending to wounds, educating the poor and forgotten in distant parts of the world. They live lives that most people would call "saintly" even though many such people do not have a place for God in their world. And, as has already been mentioned, people who profess

14. Dowd, *Queer and Catholic*. 206–7.

religious beliefs have no monopoly on virtue. The Catholic theologian, Karl Rahner, came up with the problematic term "anonymous Christians" to denote those who acted out of love and generosity even though they did not confess Jesus as Lord and motivator. It is a term that sits uncomfortably with twenty-first-century notions of self-determination and has echoes of Marx's "false consciousness". Just as the working-class proletariat did not know their own objective class-based interests, so a Buddhist monk, acting with grace and self-abandonment, might not realize that this is all possible because of the grace of God. Christ's universal reach knows no bounds. If "all things have been created through him and for him",[15] in the words of St Paul, salvation is possible for those who have never heard of the Son of God. Such views make inter-faith dialogue difficult. It falls only a tad short of a formula that goes: "you are ours even though you don't actually know it yet". If Christian orthodoxy requires that all goodness flows from God and all salvation is possible only through Christ's redemptive work, in the modern era it perhaps dictates that these views are best kept discreetly under lock and key when dealing with the three quarters of the human population on the planet that do not confess the Christian creed.

Some three weeks ago, just as I was pondering exactly on what note this restless questioning of this tsunami journey would end, another "development" akin to the tears-inducing appearance of Father Gustavo in Bajo Flores. This time, it took the form of nothing more spectacular than an email from a friend which had a YouTube video link embedded in it. "Have a look at this and see what you think. Maybe it would form the basis of a really good TV program?" he had suggested. The message had been sitting in my inbox for something like two months. I think, when it arrived, I had clicked on the video and seen that its duration was an hour and half. I have shamefully joined the legions of modern citizens for whom a video clip of anything more than ten minutes is classified as a serious inconvenience and demand on time. And of course, I had the perfect excuse: I had to finish off this book! Something else can always take precedence. The message was never deleted. It just remained there. During Advent. Then, over Christmas. The snows of January and February came and went, and the crocuses began to peer cagily above the soil on my Manchester roof terrace. Then, more than three and a half months after receiving this communication, I don't know what possessed me to do it, but one early morning in Spring, I

15. Col 1:16.

opened up my laptop and I clicked on the link entitled "God's Poet Vagabond: The Servant of God: John Bradburne".

What unfolded in the next ninety minutes was a captivating question and answer session between a man called Brian O'Neel, who hosts a channel called "That Catholic Saints Guy", and Professor David Crystal, a doyen of the linguistics world. I had read numerous books by him when training to become a speech and language therapist but had no idea he was a committed Roman Catholic.

Both men testified to a quite extraordinary man. John Randal Bradburne was born in Skirwith, a small village north of Penrith in northern England. His father, Thomas, was a committed and hard-working Anglican vicar. John was his third child, and was an uncontrollable tearaway with an obsession for climbing trees. He served out in the Far East in World War Two, was a witness to horrendous atrocities fighting the Japanese, and according to a friend, claimed to have experienced a vision of the Virgin Mary when recovering in a hospital in Medan, Sumatra after the war ended. Much to his father's chagrin, he embraced the Roman Catholic faith. John Bradburne was a restless maverick. He became enamored with the idea of monastic life and even tried his vocation as a Benedictine monk at Prinknash Abbey in the vales of Gloucestershire. But he lasted a mere four months. The life of these monks he found overregulated and allowed too little space for solitary prayer. Essentially, this man had the temperament of a hermit. In the ensuing restless years he worked as a hospital porter, a garbage collector, an assistant gravedigger, and a sacristan in London's Westminster Cathedral. He strolled the streets with his wooden recorder, which was draped in multicolored ribbons, designating himself "a jester for Christ the King", as he performed his melodies to raise money for worthy causes. Those he met spoke of his unforgettable features. Well-spoken, tall with occasionally wild hair and an irrepressible smile, John Bradburne attracted the attention of many a woman. Friends remarked that he had the face of an El Greco painting. But he was determined to consecrate his life to what the theologian Pierre Teilhard de Chardin has called the embodiment of the Eternal Feminine, Mary the mother of Jesus.

He spoke increasingly to his friends about his desire to live simply "in a cave", and when his wartime friend, John Dove, now a Jesuit priest, announced his intention to travel to Africa as a missionary, it was mooted that caves there might be a tad warmer than further north in Europe, and perhaps John should give thought to traveling out to the "dark continent".

The priest left in 1962, and Bradburne was eventually to follow him out later. He traveled to Rhodesia, which was beginning a long and painful process of racial conflict as the white minority sought to sever its ties with the United Kingdom. In resisting the calls for majority rule, it ushered in nearly two decades of spiraling violence and guerilla warfare. This was the potential powder keg that our English hermit had happened upon.

The Franciscan temperament in John Bradburne, which had been in evidence since his childhood days when he embraced his natural surroundings in Cumbria, now came totally to the fore. He resented the visits of unannounced strangers, and prayed for bees to visit him to ward off visitors. His desires were granted. This was witnessed at first hand by my former Dominican colleague, Father Colin Carr OP, in 1968 when he made visits to Silveira House, the Jesuit Mission.

"There were bees everywhere in John's abode," he told me. "He even left a clothes brush out for them on the window so that they could wipe their feet as they entered!" The Africanized bee is not your European domesticated honey-maker. Although its sting is said to be no more potent, it is much more defensive and can detect the presence of strangers and intruders hundreds of meters away. If provoked, they can counter-attack in great numbers. Destiny had led this vagabond on a convoluted journey and the following year, the tall, music-making minstrel came to understand why he had been led to such a remote and challenging part of the world.

In 1968, word reached him, via an organization called the International Medical Association, of the plight of lepers in a community in the north-east of the country. It was said to be undergoing hard times and suffering due to harsh management. Bradburne attests to being "unsettled" by this news. It nagged at him more and more until, in the end, he had to go and see for himself.

He made the life-changing expedition to Mutemwa with his close friend, Heather Benoy. They visited the leper colony at the foot of the huge granite Chigona mountain. As Bradburne's biographer attests, "the wretched creatures they encountered were repulsive, their faces and limbs deformed by a terrible disease. The lepers were covered in filth and untreated running sores."[16] There were seventy-eight members of this community. John's instant reaction on seeing them was said to have been, in words reminiscent of St Thomas, "My God, my God". The modern mind might still be shocked that leprosy, so prominent in the times of Jesus and

16. Rance, *John Bradburne*, 298.

attested to in the gospel accounts, continues to have a hold in the modern world. Known more formally as Hansen's Disease, it is caused by the bacteria *mycobacterium leprae*, which can cause damage to the nervous system, respiratory tract, skin, and eyes. In an uncanny echo of Covid-19 transmission, it is largely passed on through exposure to droplets from the nose and mouth. It has been in retreat since the 1980s and can be treated efficiently with antibiotics if detected in its early stages. But, in spite of this, there are 250,000 new cases annually worldwide, most of them restricted to India and a handful of African countries. Even the United States is not immune, with around two hundred cases reported every year.

Once he had witnessed the sight of the lepers at Mutemwa, John Bradburne ostensibly had the rest of his life mapped out for him. The wandering vagabond had found a place to engage his restless soul. Within weeks, he had become the new full-time warden of the center. "He would keep vigil with the dying person in the company of other lepers, praying and chanting with them, reading words of comfort from the Bible," according to biographer, Didier Rance. "He would struggle to fight off nausea in the hut, where the stench of putrid flesh of a leper literally rotting to death threatened to overpower him, staying on to the bitter end."[17] Bradburne went one step further than Thomas. He used his hands to touch and caress the wounds of his sisters and brothers. He was adamant in his writings that he was dealing with people of great character and beauty, and that he received great blessings from being alongside them. These encounters were to become his defining epiphany.

The "jester" had found his vocation. He did things his own way and was much loved by those he cared for. But not by the administrators who formed the committee which oversaw the governance of the center. Was it jealousy at his popularity and his growing reputation as a rather eccentric Englishman who had come to bathe the wounds of the poor and downtrodden? Petty complaints were filed against him. He was buying expensive white bread instead of brown. He was spending too much on meat rations and soap for the leper community. Personality clashes with the committee's head, William Ellis, came to a head. After more than three years in charge, John Bradburne was ordered out. Refusing to abandon his cherished lepers, he set up residence in a meager windowless tin hut at some three hundred paces from the perimeter of the camp. As an authorized Minister of the Eucharist, he was only allowed into the premises to give out the Blessed

17. Rance, *John Bradburne*, 348.

Sacrament and attend to the dying. The governing committee actually went to the lengths of applying a formal restriction order. But John Bradburne was not deterred. He was staying put.

Bradburne, the gifted musician, was also a most prolific composer of poetry. More than five thousand works exist in his name, which secured for him a Guinness World Records entry for the most published poet in the English language (173,000 lines of verse at the last count, ranging from reflections on the Holy Trinity, the beauty of eagles, to the discomforts of constipation!). And amongst the myriad of works on religious themes, he scribed poems ceaselessly about the leper community:

> This people is preeminently strong,
> A towering example, great in faith
> That has been substance of their lives so long
> As worldsong has receded like a wraith;
> Proud that their pride is beaten down to naught,
> Tremendous in their lowliness unfeigned
> And patient to a point of iron, wrought
> Truly by Lord of it whose love has reigned;
> As to their orisons and psalms and hymns,
> Persuasive these to such a high degree
> (Tuneful not very) that like pious whims
> Are those of most of us: to theirs the key
> Turns early in the gate of Paradise.
> Oft taken as by storm and in a trice.
>
> Mtemwa is a paradox, a ground
> For dogs like pariahs and men like ghouls,
> Fully equipped it is with fowls but fools
> Are few here save in Christ where they abound;
> Long lazy days spend many on their backs,
> Leisure's a pleasure they are slow to mar
> And quick to recognize, these lepers are
> Light-minded oft where soft abundance lacks;
> The ground is hard whereon they love to lie
> Lingering over noon, and after dark
> Their beds may know much heaviness, yet hark
> A passer may to psalms neath starlit sky:
> As place a paradox, in grace as fit
> As any to embrace the God of it.[18]

18. Bradburne, *The Lepers of Mtemwa* (extract).

By the mid 1970s, Rhodesia, now perceived internationally as a pariah state on account of Ian Smith's Unilateral Declaration of Independence some ten years before, was in the grip of a full-blown armed insurgency by the two nationalist parties ZAPU and ZANU. Mutemwa in the north-east became gradually encircled and in the firing line of opposing forces. Security could not be guaranteed. The maverick poet refused to countenance warnings to flee and escape the near-certain oncoming bloodbath. His loyalty to the lepers was so pronounced that he even prayed to be afflicted by the disease himself.

By September 1979, the die was cast. His reputation by this stage as a heroic and near-saintly individual had spread far and wide but it was not enough to save him. He became embroiled in a tangled web of power politics between local mujibhas (go-betweens who carried vital information between the local population and the guerillas) and the advancing insurgents. At midnight on September 2 he was abducted, led away into the night, and made to march six miles. There were trumped-up accusations that he was a spy, using a radio to pass on information to the Rhodesian military. In scenes eerily similar to the gospel accounts of Christ's passion, he was jeered and mocked. He stayed largely silent in front of his accusers. It was suggested he take the chance to escape to neighboring Mozambique, but he was defiant. He would not desert the leper community. It was Mutemwa or bust. He began the journey back accompanied by guerilla forces. A short distance into the return trip, a guerilla commander emptied the contents of his Kalashnikov into John Bradburne's defenseless body. Hours later, a close friend, Father David Gibbs, discovered him. "John was lying half-on and half-off the tarmac on the left-hand side of the road, dressed only in his underpants. He had wounds in his legs and the lower part of his chest."[19]

John Bradburne's funeral took place on Monday, September 10. This was the same day that the Lancaster House peace talks over the future of what was to become independent Zimbabwe took place in London. Even death did not bring an end to the remarkable sense of the strange, inspired, and unusual which was always near to hand in the incident-packed life of this man from humble Skirwith in rural Cumbria. At the close of the funeral service in Salisbury at the Cathedral of the Sacred Heart, several people pointed to drops of blood lying under the coffin. A purificator was sent for to mop it up, but the scene caused much consternation. John Bradburne's body had been in a mortuary and refrigerated for several days. Furthermore,

19. Rance, *John Bradburne*, 452.

blood congeals very quickly, so what was this small pool of blood under the coffin? It was subsequently taken back to the funeral parlor and opened by the funeral director himself, William Hamer-Nel, in the presence of clergy. There was no trace at all of blood anywhere inside the coffin.

It will come as no surprise that it did not take long for voices to be raised in favor of the cause for John Bradburne's beatification and canonization by the authorities in Rome. It can be a long and arduous process, and the evidential hurdles that must be surmounted are not insubstantial. But in 2019, he was declared a "Servant of God" by the Holy See, the critical first step which suggests his life is under active investigation as a possible stepping-stone towards becoming Zimbabwe's first officially recognized saint.

Why this significantly lengthy digression to consider the life of such a man? We have moved from calamity on the waters of the Indian Ocean to a story of an eccentric poet, hermit, and befriender of lepers in landlocked Africa. What links St Thomas, that story of Professor Philip Clayton and his return to faith when faced with overwhelmingly urgent human need, and the words of John Bradburne on viewing the deformities of the women and men who were to become his dearest companions? The same formula of words: "My Lord and my God." There can be no neat answer and riposte to the intellectual conundrums of that theodicy contradiction, when examined purely as a quest for simple explanation. But faced with suffering, those who respond with selfless generosity arouse in us, *in our deepest human dimensions*, a sense of awe, a sense of wonder. And when it is inspired and done in the name of he who became the ultimate victim, I cannot help but be drawn in. Such lives. Are they pointers, windows into another dimension from our vantage point of "looking through a glass darkly", in the words of St Paul?

Whatever else, this language of love only causes the most militant atheist and the troubled believer to enjoy a short-lived unity of purpose and fall silent. Such lives hit a deep, deep nerve.

In the words of T.S. Eliot, rare lives such as those of the likes of John Bradburne fulfil a distinct spiritual purpose. In one of his mesmerizing *Four Quartets*, he writes:

> to apprehend
> The point of intersection of the timeless
> With time is an occupation for the saint—
> No occupation either, but something given
> And taken, in a lifetime's death in love,
> Ardour, selflessness and self-surrender[20]

20. Eliot, *The Dry Salvages*.

Can we speak of such exceptional lives pointing to Truth and not just truth? Forgive the deeply unfashionable lapse in this post-modern world to hints at absolutes, but the Platonic strains in me cannot resist the hope that such beckoning instills in me. This is not counting the mass of human lives of mediocrity on the beads of some existential abacus. It takes only one Saint Oscar Romero or John Bradburne to comfort the oppressed (and oppress the comfortable). These pitifully few but exemplary lives can and occasionally do yank a few of the mass of humanity from the status of interested but fearful bystanders to lodestars in their own right.

If the Christian faith is in retreat in certain parts of the world, it is not because of the assaults of the New Atheists such as Dawkins, Hitchens, and Dennett. It is not because of the murderous actions of ISIS that are emptying the Middle East of many of its Christian citizens, serious as this is as a development. No, if blame must be apportioned, it is to comfortable, middle-class, nominal Christians. People like me (and perhaps you too?) who tame the urgency of the gospel demands, sanitize that demand to carry the cross, and export our obligations to serve as radical disciples to the likes of John Bradburne. Let's face it, most of us resemble all too well the dozy, fleeing disciples in Gethsemane. The amazing thing is, when all is said and done, if the Easter message holds true, that will not be enough to separate us from the love of God made known in his resurrected son.

I thought that my tsunami journey, which started with my father's uncharacteristic outburst on December 26, 2004, had ended with the final concluding words of that television documentary. But the mind never stops churning away and the heart is restless, because God's spirit is alive in the world. It turns out that there was more, much more, to say and reflect on. One of the greatest texts in the theodicy field was written by the previously mentioned Anglican vicar, Austin Farrer. His *Love Almighty and Ills Unlimited*, published as long ago as 1962 is, for some, still the unrivalled text in the troubling territory of God and Evil. Its one-hundred-and-eighty-plus pages are always engaging. I wish Farrer was still around, as there is much on which I would wish to take issue with him. But there is a stark warning on its penultimate page, words that have now been burnt into my mind, I suspect, forever:

> The inquiring mind is not to be turned back from its chosen path.
> Speculative questions deserve speculative answers . . . Peasants and
> housekeepers find what philosophers seek in vain; the substance
> of truth is not grasped by argument but by faith. The leading of

God through evil out of evil and into a promised good is acknowledged by those who trust in his mercy.[21]

So, going against the habit of a lifetime of sixty-plus years, I am going
to resolve to pray more and scrutinize less—just in the interest of restoring
some kind of balance. This western male needs to make some adjustments
and not give quite so much ascendancy to that left hand side of the brain.
This is not anti-intellectualism. The Dominicans left their stamp on me.
This is no time to abandon St Anselm's *Fides Quaerens Intellectum*, the path
to faith *through* the instrument of human reason. But it is a continuing
search for equilibrium—one that has so far proved elusive. And in that
spirit, I cannot possibly allow myself the final word. That must I leave to a
much beloved and favorite poet.

> I believe we shall in some manner be cherished by our Maker—
> that the One who gave us this remarkable earth has the power still
> farther to surprise that which He has caused.
> Beyond that all is silence.[22]

21. Farrer, *Love Almighty*, 187.
22. Dickinson, *Letter to Louise.*

Bibliography

Adams, Marylin McCord, and Robert Merrihew, eds. *The Problem of Evil*. Oxford: Oxford University Press, 1990.

Allen, Jr., John L. "When the pope's palace became a refugee center and neonatal unit." *Crux* (October 21, 2014).

Augustine. *Confessions*. Translated by Richard Pine-Coffin. London: Penguin Classics, 1961.

Barrow, John and Tipler, Frank. *The Anthropic Cosmological Principle*. Oxford: Oxford University Press, 1985.

Bowker, John. *The Problem of Suffering in the Religions of the World*. Cambridge: Cambridge University Press, 1970.

Bradburne, John, "The Lepers of Mtemwa," (1971). In "John Bradburne Poems," http://www.johnbradburnepoems.com/public/FoundPoems.aspx?poem=BRAD3257&uid=21-05-23-16-57_18&det=1.

Broad, William, *New York Times*, Science Section, January 11, 2005.

Clayton, Philip and Knapp, Steven. *The Predicament of Belief*. Oxford: Oxford University Press, 2011.

Darwin, Charles. "Letter of Correspondence to John Hooker 1856." In Burkhardt, Frederick and Smith, Sidney, eds. *The Correspondence of Charles Darwin 1856–1857*. Cambridge: Cambridge University Press, 1990.

Davis, Edward B., "The Motivated Belief of John Polkinghorne." In *First Things* (July 17, 2009). https://www.firstthings.com/web-exclusives/2009/07/the-motivated-belief-of-john-polkinghorne.

Dawkins, Richard. *The God Delusion*. London: Bantam Books, 2006.

Dostoevsky, Fyodor. *The Brothers Karamazov*. Translated by R. Pevear and L. Volokhonsky. New York: Penguin Vintage Classics, 1992.

Dickinson, Emily. "Letter to Louise and Francis Norcross." In *Letters of Emily Dickinson*. London: Everyman, 2011

Dowd, Mark. *Queer and Catholic: A Life of Contradiction*. London: Darton Longman and Todd, 2017.

Bibliography

Eliot, Thomas Stearns. "The Dry Salvages." From *The Four Quartets. Collected Poems 1909–1962*. London: Faber and Faber, 1974.

Esfahani, Ali Nadar. "Keep On Saying My God Is Great," 2003. In Berberian, Manuel. *Earthquakes and Coseismic Faulting on the Iranian Plateau*. Oxford: Elsevier, 2014.

Farrer, Austin. *Love Almighty and Ills Unlimited*. London: Collins, 1962.

Hanh, Thich Nhat, and Kapleau, Philip. *Zen Keys: Guide to Zen Practice*. New Delhi: Three Leaves, 2005.

Heidegger, Martin. *Sein and Zeit*. Translated by John Macquarrie. Eastford, CT: Martino Fine Books, 2019.

Hick, John. *Evil and the God of Love*. London: Palgrave MacMillan, 1966.

Hughes, Gerard J. *Is God to Blame? The Problem of Evil Revisited*. Dublin: Veritas, 2008.

Leibniz, Gottfried Wilhelm. *Essays of Theodicy on the Goodness of God, the Freedom of Man and the Origin of Evil*. London: Open Court Publishing, 1988.

Lennox, John. *Where is God in a Coronavirus World?* Epsom, UK: Good Book Company, 2020.

Martin, Fr. James. "Nine Reasons to Pray." In *The Tablet* (February 4, 2021).

McCabe, Herbert. *God Matters*. London: Bloomsbury, 1996.

Murphy, Nancey, et al., eds. *Physics and Cosmology: Scientific Perspectives on the Problem of Natural Evil* Volume 1. Notre Dame: University of Notre Dame Press, 2008.

Ormsby, Eric Linn. *Theodicy in Islamic Thought*. Princeton: Princeton University Press, 2014.

Phillips, Dewi Zephaniah. *The Problem of Evil and the Problem of God*. London: SCM, 2004.

Plantinga, Alvin. *God, Freedom and Evil*. Grand Rapids: William B Eerdmans Publishing Co, 1974.

———. "Good, Evil and the Metaphysics of Freedom." In *The Problem of Evil*, edited by Adams, Marylin McCord and Adams, Robert Merrihew, 85. Oxford: Oxford University Press, 1990.

The Holy Qur'an. Translated by Abdullah Yusuf Ali. Ware: Wordsworth Editions, 2000.

Rance, Didier. *John Bradburne the Vagabond of God*. Translated by Malachy O'Higgins. London: Darton Longman and Todd, 2017.

Rolston, Holmes III. *Science and Religion: A Critical Survey*. New York: Random House, 1987.

Russell, Robert John, "Physics, Cosmology, and the Challenge to Consequentialist Natural Theodicy" In *Physics and Cosmology: Scientific Perspectives on the Problem of Natural Evil* Volume 1, edited by Nancey Murphy et al., 123. Notre Dame: University of Notre Dame Press, 2008.

Sacks, Jonathan, "God and the Holocaust," https://rabbisacks.org/holocaust/topic1/.

Schillebeeckx, Edward. *Christ: The Christian Experience in the Modern World*. London: SCM, 1980.

Southgate, Christopher. "Essays in Honour of Christopher Southgate: Response with a Select Bibliography." In *Zygon* Vol. 53, No. 3, 2018.

———. *The Groaning of Creation: God, Evolution and the Problem of Evil*. London: Westminster/John Knox, 2008.

———. "Cosmic Evolution and Evil" In *The Cambridge Companion to the Problem of Evil*, edited by Meister, Chad V. and Moser, Paul K. Cambridge: Cambridge University Press, 2017.

Swinburne, Richard. *The Coherence of Theism*. Oxford: Oxford University Press, 1977.

Voltaire, François. *Candide*. Translated by Theo Cuffe. London: Penguin Classics, 2006.

Bibliography

Weil, Simone. "A Profession of Faith." In *Bilingual Essays*, edited by Gerald A. Buss. CreateSpace, 2017.

Wittgenstein, Ludwig. *Remarks on Colour*, edited by G. E. M. Anscombe. Oxford: Blackwell, 1977.

Wittgenstein, Ludwig. *Tractatus Logico-Philosophicus*. London: Routledge, 1981.